Lighthouse Keeping

A book about how God miraculously turned a hotel on the New Jersey shore into a spiritual lighthouse where the light of His presence brightly shines.

To God be the Glory Love in Him Joyce Coffin

The Logan Hotel–a "...place where I have chosen to cause My name to dwell" (Neh. 1:9).

Joyce A. Coffin

Take note that the name satan and related names are not capitalized. We choose not to acknowledge him, even to the point of violating grammatical rules.

Companion Press
P.O. Box 310
Shippensburg, PA 17257-0310
Internet: http://www.reapernet.com

"Good Stewards of the
Manifold Grace of God"

ISBN 1-56043-220-9

For Worldwide Distribution
Printed in the U.S.A.

First Printing: 1999 Second Printing: 2000

Dedication

I dedicate this book to all the precious people who have passed over the Logan threshold and taken up permanent residency in the rooms of my heart.

My Heartfelt Thanks

To the Lord who continues to do "exceedingly abundantly" more than I could ever ask or think (see Eph. 3:20 NKJ).

To my steadfast husband Larry, who has shared my vision for *Lighthouse Keeping*, for his unconditional love, selfless devotion, encouragement, wisdom, determination, and unprecedented patience through the whole process of writing this book, which is "His story."

To Emily McDermitt for her love for the Lord and the Logan, which shines forth from her artwork on the front cover.

To Carol and Kaye Clements, our covenant friends who have truly "laid down their lives for their friends" (see Jn. 15:13), for their tireless editing and Scripture proofing of the manuscript, not to mention their helping with the upkeep of the Logan for almost 20 years. To Carol, also, for drawing the lighthouses for this book. Carol has been my prayer partner and has worked with me in the Logan vineyards teaching and mentoring hundreds of girls over the years.

To Suzie and Oris Davis, our treasured friends, for their prayers, support, encouragement, and additional help with the proofreading of this manuscript. They've selflessly given up their spring weekends for the past 20 years to get the hotel "up to snuff." To Suzie, who has also typed and run labels and who has been our devoted "administrative assistant."

To my family for their love, prayers, and support while I "birthed a book."

To Kim and Gil Gotiangco for their generous gift of the computer and for their love and support.

To the wonderful guests who keep coming back to the Logan year after year.

To our precious chambermaids and managers who continue to go the "second mile" at the Logan and to their parents who have entrusted them into our care over the years.

To Marlene Bagnull, my teacher at the 1997 Florida Christian Writer's Conference, who provided a godly example of "a writer after God's own heart" and who encouraged me to fulfill my 20-year dream of writing a book about the Logan.

To Dotty Schmitt and Lydia Little, my spiritual teachers and mentors. These women of incredible faith have tirelessly poured God's Word into me for more years than I can count.

To Destiny Image and Companion Press—including Cathy Nori, Don Nori, Jr., and Jeff Hall—for their sensitivity to hear from God on my behalf and their willingness to give *Lighthouse Keeping* a chance to become a reality!

And last but not least, to our "family group" and all the other friends and family members who have helped over these 27 years to make the Logan what it is today.

Contents

Foreword

In 1979 my wife, Carol, and I moved to New Jersey after having spent 13 years in Hawaii and California. In the past, when we lived in the East, we had often vacationed at the Logan in Ocean City, New Jersey. It was a 23-room resort hotel run by Henry and Helena Meyer, a hardworking German couple who always made us feel like part of their family. In fact, Carol had vacationed at the Logan with her parents from about the age of 10. So we were eager to find out what had happened to our favorite hotel and to the Meyers while we'd been gone. The following spring we drove to Ocean City.

Imagine our delight when we discovered that the Logan was still there and still looking pretty much as it had back in the '60's. But there was an intriguing addition: a new sign on the stairs leading up to the front porch, illustrated with a descending dove, a symbol of the Holy Spirit. While living in Hawaii, Carol and I had a life-changing experience with Jesus Christ and had come to rely on the Holy Spirit to direct our lives. With anticipation we climbed the stairs.

In the lobby, which was adorned with Christian plaques, we met Joyce and Larry Coffin, who told us they had bought the Logan from the Meyers and were now running it as a Christian hotel. We quickly became friends, although I soon discovered that almost everyone who entered the main door of the Logan was treated as a friend, and even a part of the family. The warmth and homeyness of Henry and Helena Meyer was still there, yet somehow it had been enhanced by the Coffins' Christian spirit. The Logan became our family vacation retreat for the ensuing summers.

Over the years, Joyce and Larry have shared many wonderful stories of how God has been at work, not only in their lives, but also in the lives of people who have stayed or worked at the Logan. How wonderful that Joyce has now put many of those inspiring stories on paper, so that future guests and friends will be able to learn that God is concerned and works in the everyday details of our lives.

Here is the story of a simple housewife and mother who, with no prior experience, was suddenly thrust into the responsibility of managing a resort hotel while her husband continued his government job to help pay the bills. It is the story of a woman who has had to rely totally on God, and who learned how to do that by entrusting Him with even the smallest needs in her life. As a result, He was able to use her to minister to the people who came through her door. This book shows how many of those lives have been touched and changed and how their hearts have been turned toward God.

When asked which was the greatest commandment, Jesus said, " 'Love the Lord your God with all your heart and with all your soul and with all your mind and with all your strength.' The second is this: 'Love your neighbor as yourself' " (Mk. 12:30-31a NIV). This book shows how Joyce Coffin is living those words.

Harold Hostetler
Roving Editor
Guideposts Magazine
April 1999

Introduction

Again therefore Jesus spoke to them, saying, "I am the light of the world; he who follows Me shall not walk in the darkness, but shall have the light of life" (John 8:12).

Becoming an innkeeper was the furthest thing from my mind. In high school, I was never voted the "most likely" to become one. All I ever wanted to be was a wife and mother. Larry and I met when we were 15. As corny as it may sound in this day and age, it really was love at first sight! We were married three and a half years later, on December 20, 1958. Being married to Larry Coffin was a dream come true. Our firstborn, Lawrence "Chip" Kirk Coffin, Jr., was born in 1963, followed 22 months later by Kristi Ann Coffin, who was born February 14, 1965. I had the privilege of being a stay-at-home mom in our little "love nest" in Silver Spring, Maryland. Larry worked three jobs to enable me to do so. (Now, I realize that this is beginning to sound a little like "Ozzie and Harriet"....)

We didn't know at the time that the Lord had something very different in store for us. In the fall of 1972, my wonderful, athletic, pole-vaulting husband took a giant leap of faith that landed us in the hotel business. Our "new and expanded" love nest had 23 rooms, 3 apartments, and 19 bathrooms!

We entertain approximately 2,000 guests each summer. Since we became innkeepers, more than 300 teenage girls have lived in the attic and worked as chambermaids and managers. In light of all that has happened, I must say that the past 27 years have been the most meaningful, fulfilling, spiritually uplifting, difficult, and faith-stretching times of my life.

The Lord never ceases to amaze me! He took a very ordinary family and placed us in an ordinary hotel on the New Jersey shore and has done some very extraordinary things! God miraculously turned the Logan Hotel into a spiritual lighthouse where the light of His presence brightly shines. This has not been our doing; we only stand by and witness great evidences of His loving faithfulness year after year.

In April of 2000, I will celebrate my sixtieth birthday. I've come to realize, at this juncture of my life, that God will never call me to do anything unless He also equips me for the task. (No matter how overwhelming that task may seem at the time!) Through the growing pains, I began to see Jesus in a new light, and it was love at first sight! His Word has become "...a lamp to my feet, and a light to my path" just like it says in Psalm 119:105. It's such a relief to know that God is the owner of the Logan and that Larry and I are just the innkeepers.

Twenty years ago, when I was walking on the boardwalk in Ocean City, New Jersey, I said, "Lord, if I ever write a book about the Logan, what title should I use?" *Lighthouse Keeping* immediately came to mind. (I knew that it hadn't come from me!) Since that time, without even knowing it, others have referred to the Logan as a lighthouse as well! I continue to be amazed!

Now the time has come to publish a book with His title. What a joy it has been to dig out these treasures from my dusty journals. As I read and remembered, God's light shone forth from every page. I pray that as you read *Lighthouse Keeping* the warm glow of God's presence will illumine a deeper awareness of how much He wants to be intimately involved in the lives of His children.

The first four chapters lay the groundwork for the rest of the book. They tell how we first came to get acquainted with the Logan, how the door miraculously opened for us to buy it, and how the first summer brought me to my knees to accept Jesus as the Lord of my life.

The chapters that follow cover the whole spectrum from heartthrobs and sobs to quivers and shivers to guests and giggles and hilarious hotel happenings.

Sprinkled between the chapters are "Memories From the Attic." (These have been compiled by Larry, and they are a collection of treasured memories written by some of the chambermaids and managers who have, over the years, also learned to be keepers of God's light, which enhances the luster of the Logan's warm glow.)

It now gives me great pleasure to share the stories from the "lighthouse" that have been written on the tablet of my heart for so many years. To God be the glory!

"Let the Lower Lights Be Burning"

by Philip P. Bliss

Brightly beams our Father's mercy from His lighthouse evermore;
But to us He gives the keeping of the lights along the shore.

Chorus:
Let the lower lights be burning! Send a gleam across the wave!
Some poor fainting, struggling seaman you may rescue, you may save.

Dark the night of sin has settled, loud the angry billows roar;
Eager eyes are watching, longing, for the lights along the shore.

Chorus:
Let the lower lights be burning! Send a gleam across the wave!
Some poor fainting, struggling seaman you may rescue, you may save.

Trim your feeble lamp, my brother! Some poor seaman, tempest-tossed,
Trying now to make the harbor, in the darkness may be lost.

Chorus:
Let the lower lights be burning! Send a gleam across the wave!
Some poor fainting, struggling seaman you may rescue, you may save.

O send out Thy light and Thy truth, let them lead me; let them bring me to Thy holy hill, and to Thy dwelling places (Psalm 43:3).

Let the words of my mouth and the meditation of my heart be acceptable in Thy sight, O Lord, my rock and my Redeemer (Psalm 19:14).

Chapter 1

First Impressions

"For I know the plans that I have for you," declares the Lord, "plans for welfare and not for calamity to give you a future and a hope. Then you will call upon Me and come and pray to Me, and I will listen to you. And you will seek Me and find Me, when you search for Me with all your heart. And I will be found by you," declares the Lord... (Jeremiah 29:11-14).

The first time my husband, Larry, and I laid our eyes on the Logan Hotel in Ocean City, New Jersey, we never dreamed that in less than a decade it would belong to us!

This is how it all began...

Relieved to find a place to park in the loading zone in front of the Logan, Larry pulled in next to the curb and turned off the motor. The smell of salt air and the sound of the waves at the end of the street increased our excitement. We opened the doors of the station wagon and climbed out to get the full effect. It had been a long time since we had been able to take a vacation.

We welcomed the shade that this gray, five-story building provided as it loomed above us. Larry opened the rear door and reached back to unbuckle the baby. He lifted our sleeping three-month-old son, Chip, out of the car and carefully put him into my arms.

I followed him as he carried the first load up the front steps. Wicker chairs lined the front porch that wrapped around the side of the building. The white railing looked quite stark against the red carpet leading up to the entrance. Mexican ceramic tile paintings hung on either side of the jalousie door that I held open while Larry carried the suitcases into the small lobby. The hotel was so warm and homey. The smell of German cooking permeated the air.

"Velcome to the Logan," said the proprietor, appearing from behind the desk. "I'm Henry Meyer. You must be the Coffins! We've been expecting you." Then he shouted over his shoulder, "Helena, come and meet the Coffins!" A middle-aged woman joined him at the desk, wiping her hands on her checkered apron. "This is Helena, my vife," he said proudly, patting her on the back.

"Hello," Larry and I said in unison, extending our hands to the owners. I remember shaking their strong, callused hands and thinking how hard they must have worked over the years. "We're so glad to finally meet you," I said smiling. "Mom and Dad have talked about the Logan for as long as I can remember. This is their favorite place on the Jersey Shore. Are they here yet?"

"Oh, yes, they arrived a couple of hours ago. Your mom was hungry, so they vent to the boardvalk to get some pizza. Larry, the bill has been taken care of by your in-laws, so if you vill just sign the registration card I vill show you to your room."

Henry handed Larry a pen. While he registered, I walked over to one of the big front windows. The curtains billowed out as they caught the ocean breeze. Bending over so that I could see underneath the green and white awning that hung over the porch, I noticed that the entrance to the tennis courts was right across the street. Basketball courts and a football field covered the whole block between Fifth and Sixth Streets.

"You have a great location, Mr. Meyer," I said, coming back across the lobby to the desk. "Yes, ve do," Henry responded, "and the ocean is only one-half block avay, and the boardvalk is two and a half miles long! I hope you brought a stroller for the baby."

"Yes we did, and everything else but the kitchen sink," Larry teased, glancing in my direction. "Speaking of the kitchen sink, I need to carry in the rest of the things."

"Oh, don't vorry, you can leave your car there a bit longer," Mr. Meyer said, taking the card from Larry. He turned to file it in a long wooden box on a shelf behind the desk. Helena, who had been standing quietly in the background, said, "Please excuse me; I must check on things in the kitchen." We watched as Henry and his wife disappeared through the door next to the desk. Reappearing in the hallway, Mr. Meyer picked up one of the suitcases and headed for the gray carpeted steps. We followed him up the narrow staircase to the third floor, trying not to hit the antiqued railing or walls with our suitcases.

"There sure are a lot of steps in this place," I said breathlessly. Chip started to stir on my shoulder. I was grateful that he wasn't any heavier than he was. I glanced down the dimly lit hallway as we reached the landing to the second floor. The rows of dark wooden doors held a certain mystery about them. I was intrigued by this grand old place called the Logan Hotel.

"Have you had a good year?" asked Larry, a little breathless himself.

"Oh, yes," Henry smiled, "Ve alvays do. The Fourth of July veek is alvays full. By the vay, the firevorks are scheduled for tomorrow night. They shoot them off right here at the end of Sixth Street. You can sit on the front steps and vatch them from there if you vant to."

"It sounds like fun," Larry answered.

"You might vant to protect your baby's ears, though; they are very loud," offered Mr. Meyer. He took a big ring of keys out of his pocket and unlocked the door that led to the adjoining rooms.

"And I thought my key ring was large!" Larry remarked, running his hand over the old dark woodwork. "How old is the Logan? Are you the original owners?" (I could tell my husband was really interested.)

"I believe it vas built just after the turn of the century. Ve bought it almost 20 years ago. It had several owners before us."

The adjoining suite was nicely decorated. The furniture was antiqued in gold leaf. A colorful, homemade braided rug doubled as a bath mat in the shower area. (*Probably made by Helena*, I thought to myself.) Mom and Dad's things were already hung in the closet.

Passing through the door to the adjoining room we saw a nicely made double bed, a gold-leafed dresser, and a little "porta crib," complete with a homemade baby blanket over the side rail. There was a sink in the corner of the room with old-fashioned spigots. Multicolored towels hung neatly on racks above it. I put Chip down on his tummy and placed the pacifier in his mouth. He snuggled under the covers and went back to sleep. It had been a long day. Sliding the gray accordion door to one side the men put the suitcases on the floor of the small closet.

"Vile I am up here on the top floor, vould you like to see the attic?" Henry asked. (I think he was pleased that Larry and I liked the place so much.)

"We'd love to. But will Chip be okay here?" I asked.

"Don't vorry," said Mr. Meyer, "you'll hear him. It's an old place, and the sound really travels. Besides, ve vill lock the door behind us. Come vith me."

We followed him down the hall to what seemed to be a hidden passageway. Turning the corner, we carefully climbed up the ladder-like steps holding tightly onto the wooden railing. What we saw was amazing.

Beautiful wooden beams seemed to form an archway into another world. It had the feeling of a quiet sanctuary as we walked the length of the attic. Windows on every side provided a breathtaking view of the rooftops and the surrounding area. The ocean and boardwalk could be seen clearly from five stories up. Boy, did we welcome the cool ocean breeze after the four-hour drive from Maryland.

"See those beds over there?" Henry pointed to some heavy metal cots (the only "heavy metal" that has ever been allowed at the Logan to this day) and old mattresses piled under the eaves. "I vould rent them out to the servicemen for one dollar a night during the Var."

"My granddaughters, Heidi and Chrystal, stay up here now. They help us vith the chambermaiding."

"That's wonderful. I'm sure you need a lot of help with a place like this," Larry said, pounding on one of the wooden rafters with his fist. "It's built like the Rock of Gibraltar!"

"You've taken such good care of the Logan," I said. "Do you stay here in the winter?" (I had so many questions and I welcomed the chance to ask them.)

"Oh, no, Helena and I go back to Germany for part of the vinter, and sometimes ve vacation in Mexico. The rest of the time is spent vorking on the Logan getting it ready for the next season."

"Mr. Meyer, how did the Logan get its name?" Larry asked.

"The Telford to the right of us and the Logan vere named after places in Pennsylvania, I've been told."

Glancing at his antique pocket watch, Henry said, "I had better get back downstairs. Ve are expecting several more check-ins before dinner. Be careful coming down the steps now. Come down backvards. It's much safer."

We backed down the narrow steps and walked the short distance to Rooms 20 and 21.

"Thanks for the tour, Mr. Meyer," I said as Larry pulled the key out of his pocket and opened the door. As he went in to check on Chip, I turned to watch Mr. Meyer hobble down the stairs. His shoulders were stooped over. I wondered if it was from making so many beds.

Chip was wide awake and ready for a bottle by that time. After feeding him, we made our way down the four short flights of stairs to the lobby. We waited there while Larry went to find a parking place. I realized for the first time that the T.V. was sitting in the fireplace! A flowered sectional sofa to the left of the reservation desk hugged the kidney-shaped coffee table. *Henry's been busy antiquing more than just furniture*, I thought as I looked at the rest of the woodwork in the room. A small desk sat in the front corner between two windows, and several inviting easy chairs were arranged around the room. Hummel figurines peeked out from every nook and cranny. The recessed lighting made pastel green and pink patterns on the ceiling, giving a cozy glow to the rest of the room.

"Let's go find Daddy," I whispered in Chip's ear, as I carried him out onto the porch and down the steps to the sidewalk. We were just in time. Larry was just getting back from parking the car behind the high school at the corner of Sixth and Atlantic.

"I love this place," I said, running up to meet him. We put the baby in the stroller that we had hidden behind the steps for safekeeping. The Meyers had cement elves and ducks under the steps for decoration. Chip squealed with delight when he first saw them. After a few moments, we walked down the sidewalk and up the ramp to the boardwalk.

"It looks so crowded; I hope we can find my Mom and Dad!" I said excitedly. We turned the corner and joined the mass of moving people. "Hey, Larry, look at the sky. It looks as if God painted the pink and turquoise sunset with a feather duster."

He nodded; then, totally changing the subject, he said with a certain air of nostalgia, "You know, Joyce, I feel at home here already." (We never dreamed how prophetic that statement really would be.)

We had a wonderful time with my parents at their "favorite place." We enjoyed the fireworks at the end of Sixth Street and our time together at the beach. We filled a baby bathtub with ocean water and took pictures as our firstborn splashed around under the beach umbrella.

Kristi was born a year and a half later. For nine consecutive years, our little family of four stayed in Apartment A at the Logan Hotel. At the end of each stay, Larry would always say the same thing. "Mr. Meyer, if you ever decide to sell this place, let me know!"

And every year, for nine consecutive years, as we waited for the drawbridge to come down so we could cross back over to the mainland, I would comfort myself by saying, "He's got to be kidding...!"

Chapter 2

The Open Door

A wide door for effective service has opened to me, and there are many adversaries (1 Corinthians 16:9).

As I go back down the corridors of my memory, I recall that day in the fall of 1972 like it was yesterday. The phone rang and I ran to answer it, thinking it might be Larry. A familiar voice was on the other end. "Hello! This is Henry Meyer. Is Larry there?"

"No, Mr. Meyer, he's still at work. May I have him call you?"

"Yes, please, it's very important. My number is 609-399-9734. I'll be vaiting for his call," he said.

"I'll have him call as soon as he gets in. Thanks for calling!"

"Thank you, Joyce. Good-bye."

With the click of the receiver, I gasped, "I'm afraid to even imagine what this is all about." I busied myself in the kitchen and made cookies for the children for their after-school snack.

Larry took longer than usual to get home that night. The children and I greeted him at the door. Chip and Kristi were always excited to tell their Daddy about their day. I hated to stifle their enthusiasm by interrupting.

"Larry, Henry Meyer called this afternoon. He's very anxious to talk to you. The number is on the kitchen counter."

"Henry called?" Larry said with a puzzled look. "I'll call him right away." Larry put his briefcase down in the foyer and walked across the kitchen to the phone.

My heart pounded harder as I put dinner on hold and tried to piece together the one-sided conversation. Fear gripped my heart. *Henry couldn't have taken Larry seriously all those years when he asked him to let him know if he ever decided to sell the Logan!* I thought he'd been kidding!

My fears were realized when Larry hung up the receiver. "Henry said, 'I'm ready to sell, are you ready to buy?' "

"Larry, there is no way that we can buy the Logan," I said emphatically.

"Now Joyce, the first thing I need to do is try to find financing. I may not be able to. Let's pray that if God wants us to buy the Logan, He will open the door, and if not, then He'll close it."

Now, we only prayed for big things in those days. This one definitely fit into the "big" category! Larry took my hand, and I reluctantly bowed my head. He prayed, "Lord, open the door if You want us to have the Logan. You know best. If You want us to buy it, please help me to find the financing. Amen."

"There's no way," I whispered under my breath. (And to think I had thanked Mr. Meyer for calling!)

Several days later, my very disappointed husband called Ocean City, New Jersey. I tried not to let Larry see how happy and relieved I really was.

"Hello, Henry. This is Larry Coffin. Sorry it's taken me so long to get back to you. I can't find a bank that is willing to do the financing, so I guess we will have to pass up your offer."

"Vait a minute, Larry. I vant someone who loves the Logan and who loves people to have this place. Please bring

Joyce to Ocean City so that I can discuss it vith you further," he said with his heavy German accent.

Larry agreed. I stood motionless beside him. *Could the door that seemed to be closed just moments ago be squeaking open after all?* I shuddered at the thought. One thing I did know, though, was that my emotional hinges were getting a real workout.

The autumn leaves must have been breathtaking as we drove north on I-95 from our home in Rockville, Maryland, but I was too upset to notice. "I can't believe that we are even considering such a thing," I said to Larry. "What in the world would we do with a hotel? You have a government job! The kids are only seven and nine years old!"

"Don't worry about it, Joyce. If God wants us to have the Logan, everything will fall into place. Let's just enjoy this beautiful day together. Okay?"

Larry was right. He seldom took a day off from work. The children were spending a couple of days with my parents, so we should have been enjoying the time together! I peered out the window at the beautiful panoramic view as we crossed the Susquehanna bridge. I tried to make small talk for the rest of the trip, but I sensed that he was preoccupied. Usually I say, "A penny for your thoughts," but this time I was afraid to ask.

When we arrived at the Logan, we had no trouble finding a parking place. It seemed weird to be there when the porch and lobby weren't filled with people. After greeting Henry and Helena, we followed them down the first-floor hallway to their living quarters. It was so quiet that I wondered if they could hear the beating of my heart that day.

"So this is what it looks like behind the desk," I said. (I had always wanted to know.)

Helena had prepared tea and cookies for us. Even though my stomach was in knots, I politely took a cookie from the oval flowered plate. We sipped hot tea from delicate china cups. I was tempted to read what was written on the bottom (but I didn't want to be obvious). *Made in Germany, no doubt,* I thought to myself.

Henry Meyer wasted no time in making Larry the offer that he couldn't refuse. "I vill finance it for you. I vill only charge you six percent interest. Don't vorry about a thing; the Logan vill pay for itself," he said, patting Larry on the back. "The Memorial Day veekend vill bring in enough money to pay for the utilities for the rest of the year. I vil only charge you $112,500 because ve didn't go through a real estate agent." The cost fell within the range that Larry had prayed about. (He had put out a fleece even before we knew what a fleece was!)

There was no denying it. The door had swung wide open by divine intervention and we were on our way to becoming the official innkeepers of the Logan Hotel in Ocean City, New Jersey!

Of course, I might ask two things: "If God opened the door, why were there skid marks over the threshold made by the new owner's wife?"

And, "Why do we still hear, 'But Lord!' echoing down the corridors of this old turn-of-the-century hotel?"

"But Lord...We don't know how to run a hotel!

But Lord...You know that I'm not adventuresome!

But Lord...Larry has a government job 175 miles away!

But Lord...Who in the world could help us?

But Lord...What if Larry has an accident driving back and forth every weekend?

But Lord...What if the children drown in the ocean?

But Lord...Suppose the old clientele doesn't accept us!

But Lord...Can we afford to let Mom and Dad have a room if they come to help?

But Lord...What if the money doesn't come in like Henry promised?

But Lord...What church will we go to?

But Lord...Where will we sleep?
But Lord...What will I do without my husband all week?
But Lord...There are 19 bathrooms to clean!
But Lord...We will have to sleep when strangers are in the house!
But Lord...!"

Chapter 3

Me Manage?

Those who sow in tears shall reap with joyful shouting (Psalm 126:5).

Help, Lord, there's a hotel in my lap!

It was May of 1973. Once again, we were northbound on I-95. This time we brought Kristi and Chip (now eight and ten), Mom and Dad (who would help out the first three years), and almost everything I owned (including that bushel of "but Lords" that I seemed to be clinging to).

My mind was swimming with "what ifs" and "if onlys" as we crossed over the causeway into Ocean City, New Jersey. *What are we doing?* I kept asking myself. If only Larry could stay here all week and didn't have to go back to work! *What if I can't manage being a mother and innkeeper at the same time? If only I knew how to manage a hotel!...Me manage? You've got to be kidding!*

It took many trips to carry everything into the Logan. We only had a week to unpack before the guests started to arrive for the "big" Memorial Day weekend!

Mom and Dad used Room 2 on the first floor. It was bright, cheery, and very roomy—as roomy, that is, as any room at the Logan. (They're the size of rooms that you'd find in a small, European guesthouse.)

Because we were afraid that we couldn't afford to let two rooms go, Larry and I gave up our privacy and slept on an open-up couch in the living quarters behind the desk. (It was a major thoroughfare.) Chip and Kristi shared the attic dormitory with the four chambermaids who were nice enough to come help us for the summer. (After Chip got a little older, Larry built him a bunk and closet in the laundry room.) Three chambermaids were from our church and the fourth one was a niece. We couldn't have done it without them!

It was a good thing that Mr. Meyer trained us a little before he and Helena retired to Florida. He taught us how to "vash the vindows" and "vipe" the dust balls from under the beds vith a "vet" rag, how to keep the reservation chart (about which I had many reservations at the time!), and how to use "Big Mama," the industrial-sized vacuum cleaner. He gave us a list of the guests who had come in the past. He even sent out a letter introducing us as the new owners. It was so scary seeing that in print!

That first spring we went to the Logan for a work weekend. (Over the years we have had many close friends who have continued to give up their weekends to help get the Logan ready to open.) One of my greatest concerns was how the old clientele would accept us as the new owners.

Not realizing that an older lady had dropped by to meet us one day, I came bounding down the stairs covered with paint. Two ponytails flapped like whirlybirds on either side of my head as I came in for a landing at the foot of the stairs. I introduced myself to the visibly shocked elderly woman and tried desperately to recall the principles I had learned at Margabelle Young's Finishing School (a course that I had won for baton twirling in a teen talent contest). I don't believe that lady ever came back. Feelings of inadequacy flooded in once again. I never could "manage" to be someone that I was not. I don't know why I kept trying. That lesson was a hard one for me to learn.

Dad and I managed the hotel night and day. Very seldom did we get away. I tried to keep the children busy. Chip helped with the vacuuming and insisted on being the bellboy. He would carry heavy suitcases up the stairs, bumping them on every step. He loved getting little tips for his labor. Kristi helped to dust the baseboards and got two cents for every roll of toilet paper that she put on the backs of the toilets (as needed). After a while, I got suspicious of the amount of money that she was earning. A short investigation revealed toilet paper rolls piled like building blocks on the back of each toilet. Subsequently, we changed our incentive program.

I continued to be concerned about my children being at the beach without me. Kristi had been afraid to have her face splashed in the kiddie pool at our home in Rockville, Maryland. Now that we lived at the beach, she became a fish like her brother Chip. The chambermaids promised to keep an eye on them, but this paranoid mom always imagined the worst. *What if there is a riptide? Suppose a big wave pulls them under! The girls may fall asleep and someone may kidnap them!* (My anxious thoughts were greatly multiplied within me [see Ps. 94:19].)

As you can probably tell by now, I wasn't "managing" very well. Even though Mom and Dad were a big help, the stress from such a demanding job was sweeping me under. I felt like I was drowning!

When we feel as if our circumstances are pulling us under, it is wonderful that we can turn to a loving heavenly Father who will hear and answer our prayers:

"Dear Lord, during times like these, I thank You that You keep our heads above water. You said in Your Word, 'Do not fear, for I have redeemed you; I have called you by name; you are Mine! When you pass through the waters, I will be with you; and through the rivers, they will not overflow you' (Is. 43:1b-2a). (Lord, I wish I had known this promise years ago.) Help us find comfort in Your faithfulness when fears roll over us like the waves of the sea. In Jesus' name we pray, amen."

Chapter 4

Throne Room

Thy word I have treasured in my heart, that I may not sin against Thee (Psalm 119:11).

The Lord is my strength and song, and He has become my salvation (Psalm 118:14).

Just in case you were a Logan guest that first summer and heard sobbing in the showers, it was me! Where does a frustrated innkeeper go when life gets overwhelming? I figured that if I ran the water full force, no one would notice. Sorry!

Needless to say, we wasted a lot of water in those days. I would dry my eyes, put on a plastic smile, and try to be Miss Hospitality! But beneath the thin veneer, I was full of fear.

Memorial Day weekend was a disaster. It rained, and our staff outnumbered the guests. I worried about finances. I missed my husband! We had no privacy. I couldn't go to the beach with my kids! I panicked every time the phone rang! I missed family and friends! I had trouble sleeping when strangers were in the house! In the midst of it all, spinning the wheels of self-effort got me deeper and deeper into a rut of despair.

One evening, after Mom and Dad had taken the children to the boardwalk, I climbed onto the tall stool behind the reservation desk. I welcomed a quiet reprieve after such a busy day. My eyes were drawn to a little yellow booklet that someone had left on the blotter. It was entitled *Have You Heard of the Four Spiritual Laws?*[1] Turning it over, I saw that it was put out by Campus Crusade. I had heard about the Campus Crusade kids who combed the beach in the summertime. I wondered if one of them had put it there. Knowing that the silence was fleeting at best, I wasted no time. Opening to the center of the booklet, I saw a diagram with two circles. There was a throne in the center of each one. An "S," indicating self, was sitting on the throne in the first circle, and a cross, representing Christ, was outside of the circle. Dots in disarray cluttered the inside of the circle and represented interests directed by self, which resulted in "discord and frustration."

The second circle had a cross on the throne, showing that Christ was directing the life. Self was beside the throne "yielding to Christ." The dots were in an orderly fashion around it. According to the booklet, interests were "directed by Christ" and were resulting "in harmony with God's plan." When I looked at those two circles, the light suddenly dawned. "For 33 years I have been on the throne trying to run my own life!" I said out loud, amazed at what I was seeing. Sure, I had invited Jesus to help me out from time to time when the going got rough, but I had never asked Him to take control. I had been too busy spinning my wheels of self-effort!

The following two Scriptures were written on the opposite page.

---

1. © Copyrighted 1965, 1994 by Bill Bright, *New Life* Publications, Campus Crusade for Christ. All rights reserved. Used by permission.

For by grace are ye saved through faith; and that not of yourselves: it is the gift of God: not of works, lest any man should boast (Ephesians 2:8-9 KJV).

But as many as received Him, to them He gave the right to become children of God, even to those who believe in His name (John 1:12).

I had always thought that I had to be good enough to be accepted by God. Somewhere along the line I picked up the false notion that I had to earn enough points to get into Heaven and try to impress others in the process!

I knelt down in the back room and prayed, "Jesus, come into my heart and take control of my life from now on! I am so sorry that I've been on the throne all these years. Forgive me for trying to earn my way into Heaven when You already did all the work on the cross! Thank You for forgiving my sins and loving me just as I am. Amen."

Jesus became my Savior and my Lord that day in an incredible way. Now, I had never considered myself a sinner before that. I had never thought verses like "for all have sinned and fall short of the glory of God" (Rom. 3:23) and "...while we were yet sinners, Christ died for us" (Rom. 5:8 KJV) were for me! After all, I had never committed adultery, murder, or any of the "big sins."

People even thought of me as a "good Christian." (I had thought of myself that way too.) I had perfect church attendance, taught Sunday school, sang in the church choir, was president of my youth group, worked with teenagers, and took dinners to shut-ins!

How excited I was to finally realize I was a sinner and guilty of things like jealousy, pride, selfishness, and worry. Jesus had died on the cross for me, and I could be forgiven and set free! I now saw Christ in an entirely new light. It was love at first sight!

After that day, my life changed in many ways. My standard two-second prayer, "Forgive me for my sins, thank You for my blessings, and God bless everyone," changed. I started to enjoy talking to Him. I now had an awareness that He was listening! I listed my sins and the blessings specifically. Naming specific people and problems became a big part of my prayer time. Sometimes I lost track of time as I prayed.

One of the biggest changes of all came soon after. Previously, my Bible had sat on the Bible stand for all to see, but I never read it! I had thought that a person had to take a lot of courses to learn what to believe and what to leave out for one reason or another. One day, after I asked Jesus to be on the throne of my life, I picked up the Bible and God impressed the following words on my hungry heart: "This is My Word, and you can believe it."

"The whole thing?" I asked. It was as though a whole new world was opening to me. At this point I knew without a doubt that the whole Bible was true. He wrote it so that even the most simple could understand His message of salvation. I didn't know why I hadn't seen it before!

Everything in the Bible took on a whole new light. As I read it, God started speaking directly to me. Certain passages seemed to jump off the pages at me as if they were in bold-faced print, and they would say just what I needed to hear at the time. I had found a hidden treasure! God would not only meet my needs this way, but He would give me meaningful Scriptures for others as well. Becoming a Christian in more than name only was the most wonderful thing that had ever happened to me in my whole life, and there was so much more to learn. His faithfulness and constant presence make me so glad that I got out of the way and made room for Jesus on the throne of my life that day.

Since that time in the summer of 1973:

The sobbing in the showers has subsided;

My fears have begun to fade;

I look forward to reading His love letters to me in
the Bible;
I sleep more soundly even with strangers in the house;
Plastic smiles are worn less often;
Those wheels of self-effort seldom spin (although I
still forget from time to time);
God is now in the driver's seat of my life.

"Thank You, Lord, for loving the world so much that You gave Your only Son. It is such a relief to know that it's not up to us to earn points to get to Heaven. Your love and acceptance have set us free. Thank You for being so intimately involved in our lives here on earth. It takes such a big load off of our shoulders to know that You are in control. Thank You for our new life in Christ. We fall more in love with You each passing day–in Jesus' name we pray, amen."

Chapter 5

Fear Not

Then My people will live in a peaceful habitation, and in secure dwellings and in undisturbed resting places (Isaiah 32:18).

The beach is always so beautiful as it basks in the morning sun. I loved to go down to the beach early in the morning before anyone else was awake at the Logan. I took delight in watching tiny sparkles of light dancing on the glistening sea. I drank in the beauty, hoping to quiet my fears concerning Larry and the children.

"Lord, I love You," I spoke softly.

"How much?" He seemed to say.

"Oh, a lot, Lord," I said, trying to find adequate words.

"Enough to put Larry and the children on the altar?" He asked.

Now, I was familiar with the story of how Abraham was called to sacrifice Isaac (see Gen. 22:2). He trusted God's love enough to put his only son on the altar.

I knew He wanted me to do the same with Larry and the kids. Could I trust His love enough as well?

It was like major surgery as God did a deep work inside my heart.

After much agonizing, I said tearfully, "Take them, Lord; they are Yours."

I knew that I was giving God permission to do as He wished with my family. God doesn't need our "permission," but I needed to give it. I had to trust Him with the thing that I feared the most–losing my loved ones.

Just as the walls of yesterday's sand castles are broken down by the morning's incoming tide, my fears were washed away. Wave after wave of His love set me free.

I was tested each day when my kids walked toward the beach with the chambermaids. But, I was no longer afraid. I was tested each Friday night when Larry was later than expected. Yet I wasn't afraid! I had a sense that even if something did happen to them, I could handle it with God's help. His love swallowed up my fears! With Jesus, when I faced head on the worst thing that could happen, the enemy was disarmed.

"Dear heavenly Father, the never-ending waves of Your love set us free from our strongholds of fear. May we trust You enough to entrust our loved ones to You. As we stand on the shore of each new day, may we drink in the beauty of Your Son. In Jesus' name we pray, amen."

Chapter 6

Fearfully and Wonderfully "Maid"

For Thou didst form my inward parts; Thou didst weave me in my mother's womb. I will give thanks to Thee, for I am fearfully and wonderfully made; wonderful are Thy works, and my soul knows it very well (Psalm 139:13-14).

If I were to ask you what picture comes to mind when you think of a chambermaid, do you see an ole gal wearing a faded housedress held together with safety pins, a hair net, and stockings rolled down around her bony ankles? Then, obviously, you haven't been to the Logan!

Our "Logan Ladies" are beautiful servants of the Lord. They come in all ages, shapes, colors, and sizes. They are the backbone of our business. Without them, we couldn't function!

These girls come from different churches and backgrounds. Some of them bravely come without knowing anyone ahead of time. Many new relationships are made at the Logan that have lasted for years. I stand in awe at how God handpicks the girls and even divinely inspires the scheduling to bring about the right combinations.

I think of the place where we meet for daily prayer and Bible study as the "living womb." There, at the dining room table, exciting spiritual things are birthed. Even though most of the girls come with hearts for Jesus, they usually leave with something more. Now, the Lord is the One who plants the seeds and pulls the weeds. We are the ones who reap the benefits of watching His incredible garden grow. The uniqueness of each little bud, the breathtaking beauty of every blossom, the fragrance of Jesus in the midst, are all hard to even put into words. Each summer brings a breathtaking bouquet of prizewinning beauties.

Teenage worship is the sweetest sound I've ever heard. What a joy to watch as they wash in His Word and apply His truths to their lives! He gives homework too. Part of that homework is to pray over the rooms and "work heartily, as for the Lord rather than for men" (Col. 3:23b). (I tell them to clean as if Jesus Himself were staying in each room.)

People have told me that they sleep better at the Logan than they do at home. Others have sensed God's presence in a profound way. I believe that this is because God has placed His name upon the Logan and then commissioned these beautiful young intercessors to clean His house (not only in the natural, but spiritually as well).

All our maids come bearing spiritual gifts and fruits! I'm surrounded by girls with merciful hearts, organizational skills, leadership and musical gifts, servants' hearts, and gifts of intercession (just to mention a few). They lift my arms as Aaron and Hur did for Moses when he was called to do something that he didn't feel equipped to do either (see Ex. 17:11-13). I call them my "Aarons and 'Hers' " In almost 300 chambermaids, no two have been alike—not even the twins! I'm amazed at the creativity of our awesome God. One of my favorite things is to become a job reference for them as they fly out of the Logan nest. It gives me such pleasure to tell about their godly qualities to others.

Some of them have started Bible study groups in their high schools and on their college campuses. ("I have no greater joy than this, to hear of my children walking in the truth" [3 Jn. 1:4].)

One day I asked Larry, "When you think of our chambermaids, what comes to mind?"

And with a smile of affection, the following poured out of his surrogate father's heart: "Sweet and considerate, beautiful inside and out, hardworking, fun, spiritual 'works in progress,' beautiful voices and personalities, kind of person you'd want your son to marry, 'Proverbs 31 women,' helpful, thoughtful, intelligent, trustworthy, thorough, kind, obedient, normal, sensitive, enthusiastic, teachable, love the Lord, loved by the Lord (and by us)."

If you ever happen to be an early riser at the Logan and get a whiff of graham crackers mingled with orange juice, you'll know it's coming from the "living womb." The Word of God says, "For where two or three have gathered together in My name, there I am in their midst" (Mt. 18:20). So you can also be assured that Jesus is in the "living womb" tending His "garden." The Bible says, "Awake, O north wind, and come, wind of the south; make my garden breathe out fragrance, let its spices be wafted abroad. May my beloved come into his garden and eat its choice fruits!" (Song 4:16)

These girls have known the gentle breezes of the blessings of the Lord. Some of them have experienced the cold, harsh, north winds of trial as well. The fragrance of Jesus that comes from their brokenness has blessed all those who have known them.

Once in a while, I invite a friend to share God's Word with my girls. Glenda Mills has come and shared on many occasions over the years. In closing, I would like to share something she wrote for them the summer of 1998.

"Dear Hand-Maidens of the Lord,
How beautiful are the hands that serve the Body of
Christ...
How beautiful are the feet of those who walk
And carry the love of Jesus wherever they go.
How beautiful are those who have doves' eyes;
They only see one thing at a time.
They are focused on their Lord
Who makes all things work together for good
For those who love Him.
How beautiful are the faces of the anointed of God;
They reflect the glory and the radiance of the Son.
How beautiful you are to your Beloved...and to me.
You are a 'Rose of Sharon'...each of you!"

"Lord Jesus, thank You for the beautiful young people who have been birthed into Your Kingdom. We have been blessed by Your fragrance that comes from their lives. Protect them as they take a stand for righteousness in this day and age. May their love and devotion to You be an example to all of us. They are truly 'fearfully and wonderfully made' (see Ps. 139:13-14). In Jesus' name we pray, amen."

The following passage is our continued prayer for each of the girls who remain in our hearts:

I thank my God in all my remembrance of you, always offering prayer with joy in my every prayer for you all....For I am confident of this very thing, that He who began a good work in you will perfect it until the day of Christ Jesus....For God is my witness, how I long for you all with the affection of Christ Jesus. And this I pray, that your love may abound still more and more in real knowledge and all discernment, so that you may approve the things that are excellent, in order to be sincere and blameless until the day of Christ; having been filled with the fruit of righteousness which comes through Jesus Christ, to the glory and praise of God (Philippians 1:3-4,6,8-11).

Memories From the Attic

Who would have known the summer of '91 would bring such a life-changing experience for me? God knew.

I had been spending time with another girl who had been coming to the Logan for several years, and she was persistent about selling me on what a great place the Logan was: It's at the beach; room and board are free; there's not much physical work; you can play tennis, basketball...and you practically have most of the days to yourself. I was sold, and it sounded like a fun summer job, but I had to meet this "Joyce lady" first.

Our first meeting was at the table in her kitchen, and she began by asking me about my church background and a little about my family history. Then she shared the "rules" I would have to follow while staying at the Logan. They didn't seem like anything tough to follow, but there was a little bit of an intimidating factor to face in the Logan regimen–Bible studies, prayer times, and personal devotions.

Throughout my life I've been in and out of church, always attended vacation Bible school, was occasionally a member of a youth group, went on a mission trip to Kentucky, and even attended prayer meetings at high school during my lunch period. So it wasn't that I was opposed to the "God thing." I just didn't understand it. But considering that it was accompanied by a week or so at the beach with free room and board, I decided to give it a chance. After all, it was only for a short time.

The first day was nice as I met the other "Loganettes" I would be living with and working closely with for the next week. Right away, I could tell that these were pretty mature girls. They seemed to have it together, and they were really into this "God" guy. I really started to feel intimidated, yet I was curious. Everyone made me feel especially welcome and very comfortable, but the first morning Bible study hadn't happened yet.

The next morning wasn't what I had anticipated. There was an incredibly long prayer time, but there were thanks and admiration for this Man that seemed almost human in the way that He was being addressed. The reason for this was that my new companions shared such a personal relationship with Him. Someone even thanked Him for the yucky weather. I thought, "Wow, this really is a personal thing!"

The personal devotions weren't too bad because I could go at my own pace and figure out God, Jesus, and how I would actually speak to Him as I might speak to a friend. The third day came, and the time came to pair up with someone else and pray for each other's needs or to offer praise to God for whatever came to our hearts. I wondered, "How am I going to do this when I've only ever prayed a short blessing over food when forced?" I know I stumbled a bit and was a little awkward, but I remember thinking afterwards, "That wasn't too bad!" One more obstacle lay ahead though–leading a short devotion and praying before breakfast the next morning. Praying before a room full of people who, in my opinion, had much more mature relationships with God was unnerving and quite an intimidating thought, so I practiced what I would say. I got through it, anxious as I was, and went about my everyday chores. This third day was cause for great self-reflection. I found myself constantly reading Scripture, particularly Psalm 91, and having conversations with God in my head. I was going through a difficult stage of my life at the same time, and about the middle of the fourth day, June 26, 1991, sobbing, I called out for Christ to save my life. At that point I knew that I couldn't depend on my strength, knowledge, or will. But I knew deep inside that I could trust in Christ. It's hard to explain. Someone really has to experience it to understand. I had the most incredible sense of peace and freedom at that moment.

Since that time, I have had plenty of valley experiences as well as mountaintop experiences, but through it all, the love of Christ has sustained me. His word has never failed me, and I've always known that He is there; it's a very peaceful feeling. My relationship with Christ and with His Church has become a way of life, not just a Sunday thing and not just a "going through a bad experience right now" thing. Like Joyce always says, "I'm in the college of the Holy Spirit, and I hope never to graduate." *I look forward to all the chapters God has for my life, and I'm still becoming who I am...a chosen and free child of God!*

Kim (Hendricks) Gotiangco '91-'97

Chapter 7

"We Three Kings"

Do nothing from selfishness or empty conceit, but with humility of mind let each of you regard one another as more important than himself; do not merely look out for your own personal interests, but also for the interests of others (Philippians 2:3-4).

As much as I'd like to make "A's" on all my tests, I usually fall short. It's very humbling to admit that my initial reactions are not always godly.

One test came during a particularly slow time in June. We had spent the entire day painting Apartment C. It was time to call it a day. I encouraged the girls who were there at the time to go down to the boardwalk. Trying desperately to come up with something easy for dinner, I was startled by the bell at the front desk. Suddenly, I remembered that we were expecting guests that evening. There was no time to wash up, so I appeared behind the desk spattered with paint and looking a bit haggard to say the least.

Three couples had made their way into the lobby undetected. "Welcome to the Logan," I said rather breathlessly, brushing a strand of "sunshine yellow" hair out of my eyes. "Please excuse my shabby appearance."

They all smiled politely and said, "Hello."

One of the men stepped up to the desk and put a piece of paper in front of me. "We've reserved three rooms with toilet and shower for two nights," he said. "This is the confirmation letter you sent to us last month."

I took the letter, checked the chart, and reassured him that the rooms were ready and waiting.

"By the way," the gentleman continued, "when my wife and I were here before, you pushed the twin beds together and made a king-sized bed. Would you do that for us again, please?"

"Why, sure we can," I said, trying to sound cheerful (thinking all along how much trouble it would be to unmake two twin beds and put on the king linens.)

When the other two couples heard about it, they decided that they wanted king-sized beds as well.

I said, "No problem!" (Now I was thinking how much easier it would have been to have known this ahead of time.) I finished checking the couples in. They paid their bills and then went out front to bring in their luggage from their van.

Quickly grabbing their keys, I dragged my poor paint-spattered body up the steps to start making six twin beds into three king-sized ones. *It's such a shame to disturb those beds! The chambermaids worked so hard to make them look so nice. It's like destroying works of art!* I continued to grumble in my spirit. I stomped up the next flight of stairs with my arms full of linen, and I was shocked at the question God then impressed on my heart: "Would you do it for Me?"

"Well, of course, Lord," I answered without hesitation. "I'd do it for You! But You would have been kind enough to let me know ahead of time," I said with bitterness lapping at my lips.

I was embarrassed by my resentful attitude as I stood in the presence of my King of kings. At that very moment, it was as if the Lord scooped this sin-spattered, reluctant servant into His arms of love. He reminded me that I had always been a strong supporter of good healthy marriages and loved seeing the closeness between loving couples.

I had never felt so ashamed and so loved at the same time. I'm so glad that His reprimands come wrapped in hugs! (They could be described as being kinda like "spanks" in a blanket.)

As I quickly stripped the twin beds and folded the linens, He brought this verse to mind: "...to the extent that you did it to one of these brothers of Mine, even the least of them, you did it to Me" (Mt. 25:40).

I began to pray as I worked, "Forgive me, Lord, I was thinking only of myself and not of their comfort. The next time You give me a 'king-sized' job to do, please remind me that it really is an honor to serve my brothers and sisters in Christ. Please get the old Joyce out of the way so that You can bless others in this place."

On the way back down to the kitchen, I had a little spring in my step and a genuine smile on my lips. I warmly welcomed the three couples who met me coming up the stairs.

Since that day, the following verse has been a basic part of our job description here at the Logan:

> *Whatever you do, do your work heartily, as for the Lord rather than for men; knowing that from the Lord you will receive the reward of the inheritance. It is the Lord Christ whom you serve* (Colossians 3:23-24).

Now we try to do everything here at the Logan as if He Himself were staying in each room. After all, He really is!

"Dear Lord, may we always welcome opportunities to serve others. In serving them, in essence, we are serving the greatest Servant of all. It's worth it all to hear You whisper 'Thank you'...even when others may forget! In Jesus' name we pray, amen."

Just as the Son of Man did not come to be served, but to serve, and to give His life a ransom for many (Matthew 20:28).

Memories From the Attic

I have many great memories from the Logan. As long as I can remember, my summers were spent in Ocean City, New Jersey. At the age of eight, I started my debut as a chambermaid. I earned my keep by stacking rolls of toilet paper on the backs of the toilets in every bathroom in the entire hotel. My parents gave me two cents per roll. What my parents didn't realize, however, was that I was bringing in quite a bit of money daily. After investigating, they found that I had stacked about 15 rolls per bathroom. I thought that I was being very efficient and at the same time earning money for fun on the boardwalk.

I remember always wanting to be like the "big girls," who were chambermaids and managers at the Logan. I was sure that I could do everything they did. At the old age of ten, I thought that I was as mature and as pretty as they were. One evening, after the girls gave in to my pleas to let me go with them to the boardwalk, I noticed that we were receiving some looks as we strolled along. I proceeded to inform the other girls that the boys were looking at "us." They got such a kick out of this, and to this day, they won't let me live this down!

Kristi (Coffin) Ivosevich '73-'85

I remember the very first time I cleaned a room at the Logan. Joyce was training me for my very first summer at the hotel. I don't remember what room number it was, but it was one of the easy ones–just two beds and a sink. Joyce had instructed me to dust everything. So I began dusting the light fixtures, the bed frames, the dresser top, the chair, the chair rungs, the windowsill. I think I even dusted the door! I was so excited that I had done such a thorough job of dusting that room. I was ready for my inspection!

I called Joyce to let her know I was finished. She came in and began the white-glove test. I was confident that everywhere she touched, my dust rag had been there. But then she reached above the door and wiped the top of the molding! Oh no, I had forgotten that! I don't remember Joyce's words, but I remember her gentle spirit as she encouraged me to keep cleaning for Jesus!

That is just what I did each summer from Memorial Day 1980 through 1984, the year I was married. I loved having my season as a chambermaid at the Logan. Each week began with an exciting ride with Larry as he piled us girls and all our gear into the van. He always made some comment that he thought we could have packed lighter. We all knew he was right, but we never changed our ways!

Ellen (Jones) Zell '80-'84

Chapter 8

Transformation in Room 8

Create in me a clean heart, O God, and renew a steadfast spirit within me....Restore to me the joy of Thy salvation, and sustain me with a willing spirit (Psalm 51:10,12).

Interior decorating isn't always something that simply meets the eye.

When we redecorated one of the hotel bedrooms, I never dreamed that God was setting the stage to do some extensive renovations in me!

There was no doubt about it. Room 8 needed transformation. Of all the Logan's rooms, it was the least appealing.

We had saved the moss green carpeting from our living room in Maryland for "such a time as this." It fit perfectly. Larry hung green and blue-striped wallpaper on one wall and painted the other three with sunshine yellow. (Everything was sunshine yellow in those days.) Aunt Doris and Uncle Norman had donated two gold-framed, blue-matted prints of Paris, which we carefully hung over the two twin beds. Of course, Henry Meyer's antiqued nightstand, dresser, and chair completed the decor.

"This looks great," said Emily, one of our more artistic staff who had a definite eye for color.

"Thanks for putting the finishing touches on the woodwork," I said, putting the tiebacks on the curtains. The powder blue shears danced playfully in the ocean breeze.

I backed out of the room, savoring the beautiful transformation that was taking place right before my eyes. "The people are just going to love it! Someone is coming into this room at the end of the week. I can't wait to see how she likes it."

As the days passed by, I would find excuses to take towels up to the linen closet, near Room 8, so that I could admire the work of so many loving hands.

By Thursday, my mind was filled with many other things. Meals needed to be planned for the weekend, and food needed to be bought. We had to make welcome signs for the new chambermaids who would be arriving with Larry. About mid-afternoon, I ran out to pick up a few last-minute things at the grocery store.

When I returned from running my errands, I slowly pulled into the driveway between the Logan and the Ebbie guesthouse next door. One of my managers ran out to meet me before I could get out of the car.

"Wait until you meet the lady in Room 8," she whispered, rolling her eyes. "She hates it here. She says the room is small and smells like paint. It's the 'worst room she's ever seen.' She plans to check out first thing in the morning. She's requested that we find her a motel in town."

I couldn't believe what my manager was telling me! A mixture of feelings rose up within me that was anything but a sweet fragrance to the Lord.

I can't believe this woman! Who does she think she is? I thought to myself. We went in the side door and carried the packages up the stairs to the kitchen.

The girls unpacked the groceries and put them away while I showered and changed. It was my turn to take the desk for the 5:30 to 11:00 p.m. shift. The chambermaids who were assigned to the evening meal had already started the dinner preparations.

Meanwhile, I went behind the desk to doublecheck the correspondence that had been done on the afternoon shift. It wasn't long before the atmosphere seemed to change. I looked up from what I was doing and saw a lady coming down the stairs who was looking as if she smelled something really bad!

She glared at me from under her "black cloud" and said, with her nose wrinkled up, "I hope you have been informed about how unhappy I am with my room!"

"Yes, my manager told me. I'm so sorry you don't like it here. Many people love the Logan, but I guess that it just isn't what you expected. I'd be glad to try to find you a place by tomorrow morning as you requested." (I tried to be as pleasant as I could, under the circumstances.)

Momentarily pacified, she turned in a huff and walked out the front door. It immediately became evident to me that bitterness was still brewing in my heart while honey dripped from my lips. "Lord, help me," I prayed.

The chambermaids were busy setting the table as I came into the dining room from behind the desk and said, "Girls, I need your help! I just met the grouchy lady in Room 8! The problem is, I'm loving her with my mouth but not with my heart. Please pray for me."

The girls came quickly to my rescue. We held hands and formed a little prayer circle. One by one, those precious girls prayed that God would change my heart.

After dinner, most of the people, including my staff, went to the boardwalk. Normally, I would have had time alone to get some work done. But this night was different. The lady in Room 8 decided to spend the whole evening in the lobby! She glared at me, demanding one thing after another. The light bulb needed to be replaced, she wanted another pillow and a fan and some extra towels. Each request came separately, so I was running up and down the stairs like a jackrabbit trying to accommodate her. She seemed to be enjoying the control. As odd as it may seem, as the evening wore on, I could sense a growing love for her. I actually started to enjoy doing things for this lady! It was as if I could feel God's love pouring out of my heart and washing over her. What an amazing experience that was!

Even more amazing is what happened the next day. We had finished devotions and had just started to eat breakfast when someone rang the bell at the front desk. As I rounded the corner and stepped into the office, I saw the guest from Room 8. I almost didn't recognize her without her black cloud! The lines of her face were softened as she pleaded, "Mrs. Coffin, could I possibly spend the rest of the week here? I know that I'll never find another place in Ocean City as warm as this one." (Now, I knew that we didn't have air conditioning, but somehow, I sensed that she wasn't talking about the weather!)

"Of course, you can stay here," I exclaimed, trying to contain myself as I marveled at God's transforming power. It was wonderful to watch God water her with His love that week. She was like a thirsty plant opening up to the Son.

One day, I took her downtown to do some shopping. She had originally planned to get a taxi because of her "bad legs," but I insisted on driving her myself because I didn't want to miss another "king-sized" opportunity.

She wanted to pay me. "You can't pay for love gifts," I responded.

"Well, I know what I'll do for you," she said smiling. "I'll pray for you!"

"Oh, thank you. We can use all the prayers we can get," I said, afraid to blink for fear that this had all been a dream.

The day that the lady in Room 8 checked out, she cried as she thanked me for her wonderful vacation at the Logan

Hotel! It was evident that God had touched her life in a very special way. His light had penetrated the darkness and enabled her to receive His love. (She even looked different.) Through it all, I had received a deeper revelation of how His love can miraculously change the human heart (especially my own). I know one thing for certain–from that day on, I've looked at "interior decorating" from an entirely new perspective!

"Dear Jesus, our hearts ache to be changed by You. We marvel at the transforming power of Your unconditional love. In Jesus' name we pray, amen."

Memories From the Attic

My sister, Kristen, had already been working at the Logan for two summers before I was old enough to be a chambermaid. She always wrote home about the fun and exciting times she and the other girls had. To this day, I clearly remember being jealous of her being able to work there; it seemed like such an ideal and perfect summer job. My parents and I would take a trip to Ocean City, New Jersey, to stay for a weekend and visit Kristen each summer. I can still remember the feelings I had being there and the thoughts that ran through my mind. "When will I be allowed to work here? These girls seem so cool and grown-up, and wow, they get to live at the beach!" As a new teenager, I saw the importance of the social aspect of the job rather than the spiritual or even the work part of the job. As time progressed, though, both my feelings and my attitudes changed.

The first and second summers I worked there I didn't stay for long. I went up for a few weekends and only one or two weeks. My very first time working there was considered my "training weekend," and although I don't have any specific memories of the weekend, I do remember coming away feeling as if I had found the perfect job for me! As each year passed, I worked for longer periods of time and enjoyed it more and more for so many reasons.

Jenny Parent '91-'99

Chapter 9

A Hug for Nancy

Then your light will break out like the dawn, and your recovery will speedily spring forth; and your righteousness will go before you; the glory of the Lord will be your rear guard (Isaiah 58:8).

Over the course of a summer, we check a lot of people into our hotel, but on this particular occasion, it was different. Two ladies stood on the other side of the reception desk. Only one did all the talking. The other one never made eye contact or spoke a word.

I wonder what in the world is wrong with her? I asked myself, trying not to notice.

The two unlikely friends would be with us for several days, so I needed to decide how to handle the situation. I was faced with two choices. I could ignore her and treat her like she was treating me, or I could treat her like I did all the other guests. I decided on choice number two.

"Hi, Nancy! How are you this morning? Did you sleep well? You must have...you look pretty bright-eyed and bushy tailed!" I'd say as she came down the steps into the lobby. Inwardly, I chuckled at how funny I must have sounded. After a day or two, I could get her to chuckle too, but she never spoke.

The day they were to check out came quickly. "Lord, is there a gift that I can give Nancy that would help her to know that You love her?" I prayed. Searching my room, I found a little plaque that I quickly wrapped in tissue paper. Frantically, I ran through the lobby, out the door, and down the front steps. I was relieved to see that Nancy and her friend were still packing the car in the loading zone.

"Nancy, here's a little gift for you," I said breathlessly as I handed it to her. Then, without thinking, I wrapped my arms around her and gave her a big hug right there in the middle of Sixth Street. I waved good-bye as I climbed up the steps.

A prayer of intercession arose in my heart. "Lord, You know what is wrong with Nancy. Why doesn't she talk? Why did she feel so stiff and unresponsive when I tried to hug her? She reminds me of a hurting little puppy. I'll probably never see her again, but You will. Please wrap her in Your arms of love and heal her hurts–in Jesus' name, amen."

I busied myself with hotel matters. My thoughts concerning Nancy were prayerful but always shrouded in mystery.

A few months passed by and we moved back to our home in Maryland, where we spend each winter. The mailman left a lot of mail one day. Most of the letters had been forwarded to us from Ocean City, New Jersey. One piece of mail was from someone whose name I didn't recognize. The mystery was solved when I started reading the letter.

It read something like this: "Dear Joyce, You may not remember me. I'm the lady who didn't talk. I really did love my time at the Logan Hotel last summer. You had no way of knowing but you gave me a very special 'gift' when I left. You gave me a hug. It was the first time anyone has ever hugged me in my whole life! I know now that God really does love me, and I need to get close to Him again. Thanks for letting Him love me through you. I will never forget. Love, Nancy."

I never dreamed that God would take such a small effort on my part to bring about such big results. (All along, I thought the gift was the one wrapped in tissue!) I know in my heart of hearts, that it was really God who wrapped Nancy in His love that day. He only used my arms!

"Lord, is there anyone else out there who needs a hug today? Help us to reach out to those who need Your love–in Jesus' name we pray, amen."

* * *

Update!

More than 20 years later, Nancy and I are still good friends. We continue to send each other stationary and gifts with "hugs" on them. I never cease to be amazed when I pick up the phone and hear Nancy's cheerful voice on the other end. She still loves to tell others about the healing that God's love brought in her life.

One of her favorite pastimes is to listen to praise and worship tapes. (I believe that God has used this as a powerful tool during the healing process.)

After Nancy moved away more than 15 years ago, she studied to become a medical technician. And just this past year, she graduated from Bible school.

Oh yes, Nancy continues to enjoy God's hugs now more than ever, and she gives them as well. In January, I went to a women's conference in her hometown. Nancy was at the airport to surprise me when I got off the plane. It had been almost 15 years since we had seen each other. What a great reunion we had! Her warm hug was worth the wait! If only I had remembered my camera Sunday morning when she took me to her church. I had the awesome privilege of watching Nancy, in her role as church greeter, hugging everyone who came through the door! To God be the glory for the awesome things He has done!

> *The Lord appeared to him from afar, saying, "I have loved you with an everlasting love; therefore I have drawn you with lovingkindness."..."And their life shall be like a watered garden, and they shall never languish again"* (Jeremiah 31:3,12b).

Amen!

Memories From the Attic

When we arrived at the Logan, Joyce was always on the front porch with a big smile and open arms ready to welcome the next group of chambermaids. We knew that she was so glad we had come. It wasn't the beginning of a week of work, but of fellowship! We carried our luggage up the narrow stairways to the attic. My favorite spot to sleep was in the bed next to the windows that faced the ocean. At night I could watch the lighted Ferris wheel go 'round while enjoying the cool ocean breeze. The attic was a special spot away from all the hustle and bustle of life. It was so peaceful to sit in the highest place of the hotel and yet have no one know you were there. I loved to read the Bible and pray with no distractions or other bids for my attention. The Lord met with many a chambermaid up there, I'm sure!

I learned to clean very thoroughly while I was at the Logan. I also learned to read the Scriptures with a searching heart, knowing that God would speak to me. I learned to look for **rhema** *from God, and He answered me time and time again. The priorities were set each day: First spend time with Jesus, then everything else will follow, as we live out Matthew 6:33 (KJV): "But seek ye first the kingdom of God, and His righteousness; and all these things shall be added unto you." That is one lesson I keep coming back to again and again as I try to live each day glorifying the Lord.*

Ellen (Jones) Zell '80-'84

Chapter 10

Lost Joy

If you do well, will not your countenance be lifted up? And if you do not do well, sin is crouching at the door; and its desire is for you, but you must master it (Genesis 4:7).

Have you ever heard of a "big toe" ministry? Well, in those early years, before we started having Bible studies, I would go down to the ocean first thing in the morning. The hardened beach, which had been created by the outgoing tide, became my sandy tablet. Barefooted, I would back up while dragging the big toe on my right foot (I am right-handed, so I guess I'm right-footed too!) I'd write a Scripture for the day in six-foot block letters between the ocean and the boardwalk. It became a billboard on the beach easily read by bikers and joggers.

Several mornings in a row (while I was keeping my ministry in "tow"), an Oriental lady passed by. She stopped to read the Scripture and then continued her silent walk down the beach. My eyes followed her small frame as she slowly walked away. A beach robe shrouded her stooped shoulders, and her head hung as low as her countenance. It was as if she was in mourning.

"Father," I prayed, "please help that lady. She seems so sad."

The next morning, we met again. This time she actually commented on how much the Scriptures had meant to her each day! I listened intently as she spoke softly.

"You see," she continued, with tears in her eyes, "I've lost my joy." She went on to explain that she had inherited a large estate. Material things had taken the place that God had once held in her life. I felt prompted to pray for her. I chickened out! It seemed much less intimidating to pray to myself.

I suddenly remembered a book that had impacted Larry and me in such a profound way. It was by Merlin Carothers and called *Prison to Praise*. I told the lady that I had an extra copy at the Logan and asked her to walk back with me to get it. She agreed. Once again, I felt the urge to pray. At that point, we were under the boardwalk where there was a little privacy. Once again, I pushed the prompting away.

We walked through the parking lot onto the sidewalk at Sixth Street. People were milling all around. There were bikers; dads pulling kids in wagons; and little children with buckets, eager to find special treasures on the beach.

All at once, it dawned on me that I had found a "treasure" myself!

As we dodged the crowds, I felt the undeniable desire to pray for her once again. This time the desire was so strong that I decided not to dodge it. I asked her if she would like me to pray for her. She stopped right there in the middle of the sidewalk and bowed her head. "Oh Lord," I said to myself, "if I had only prayed the first time You told me to. Forgive my disobedience."

I took her hands into mine. Closing my eyes to shut out the gawkers, I began to pray softly: "Lord, my friend wants to make You the center of her life again. She is sorry that she has put possessions before You, God. Please put a new song in her heart and fill her with Your joy once again—in Jesus' name, amen." When I was finished, she prayed a beautiful prayer asking for forgiveness. She asked God to be the center of her life once more.

My new friend and I walked the rest of the block to the hotel. What people might have thought of me didn't seem to matter anymore. She waited on the front porch while I ran into the Logan. I quickly found *Prison to Praise* and brought it out to her. Thanking me, she held it to her heart as if she too had found a treasure. We said good-bye, never expecting to see one another again. (She was supposed to go home the next day.)

Early the next morning, I went to my favorite place. Under the boardwalk, the sound of the surf drowned out my voice as I prayed out loud and sang to the Lord. My personal "tabernacle" had a cathedral ceiling. Golden rays from the rising sun made fancy patterns under my feet as streams of light poured between the cement pillars. I couldn't imagine a more beautiful place to worship than my sanctuary by the sea. The glory of God's presence was unmistakable as I marveled over the events of the previous day.

It was such a wonderful experience that I almost lost track of the time. Looking at my watch, I located a hardened place in the sand.

It's funny how we sometimes get so preoccupied with what we are doing that we become unaware of our surroundings.

I don't know how long my new friend had been standing there. Finally, I looked up. A radiant smile lit up her face. "I found my joy!" she said with a song in her voice. "I read the book before I went to sleep last night. As I praised the Lord for His goodness, He healed my broken heart and restored my joy! Before I left, I just had to let you know!"

Tears of joy filled our eyes as we rejoiced in what our heavenly Father had done.

God had used my reluctant prayer to bring a jolt of joy that surprised us both. What a wonderful God we have! I'll never forget the last time I saw her. There was such a change in her countenance. She had a new spring in her step. There was no doubt in my mind that God had become the glory and the lifter of her head (see Ps. 3:3). She had confessed her sin of idolatry, received the cleansing of the blood of Jesus, and begun to praise. Now her joy was made full (see Jn. 15:11).

"Father, help us to be willing witnesses for You. As You plant Your joy in others, it becomes our joy as well. What a treasure that is, Lord. Thank You for involving us in Your work here on earth. It makes life so exciting! We love You and eagerly wait for the next assignment! In Jesus' name we pray, amen."

All my springs of joy are in You (Psalm 87:7b).

Memories From the Attic

Joyce had a lot of mouths to feed. Even though there was an attic full of hungry teenage girls, she would still find room for some hotel guests or Ocean City residents to join us for dinners. All the hours I wasted sunbathing aren't my cherished memories; my real memories are the times spent around the kitchen table. I don't ever recall a time that we ever missed "go around the table." Once all the food was passed (which was always done systematically–take what's in front of you, then pass it to the left), Joyce would pose a question. Something like–"If you could have lunch with anyone, who would you choose?" I can still hear the laughter of many, many summers gone by as we went "around the table."

The only thing I would dread at the Logan was Room 5. This was Joyce and Larry's room, but it would manifest itself into something else if you were in trouble. On such an occasion, you would get a "Room 5 Talk." Joyce insisted that those talks were also used to share good news. This I know to be true; one time when I was called into Room 5, it was to ask me to move from my position as chambermaid to hotel manager. But I still giggle at the other ones I got much prior to that for my rowdiness. That room helped to shape many girls into mature ladies.

Gwen (Gill) Everett '80-'92

As I think about it, one of my most exciting memories was when Scott Wesley Brown came to the Logan to stay overnight. He was my favorite and most inspiring Christian musician at the time. I also remember going to the "Glad" concert. Who would have ever thought that they would become as BIG as they did in the Christian music world! Christian music has been such a blessing to me over the years. It somehow motivates you to keep on going!

One memory that has really stuck with me was Joyce's "big toe ministry"! I never forgot the lady she met on the beach who had "lost her joy"! I learned so many wonderful lessons working those summers at the Logan, but this one has been so valuable to me. I have learned to always have the joy of Jesus in my heart and to share it with others. Through so much of my life, His joy has seen me through some very difficult times and helped me to go on, especially lately with my husband Tom's debilitating illness. The joy that I am talking about is the joy that only Jesus can give. The world can't give it. It's so sad to watch people search for this joy in different ways, but they never find it until they truly know that Jesus sacrificed His life for them on the cross and rose again. Only by truly knowing Jesus can you ever have true joy in your life.

Robin (Rohr) Green '74-'78

Chapter 11

A Miracle in My Arms

But you are a chosen race, a royal priesthood, a holy nation, a people for God's own possession, that you may proclaim the excellencies of Him who has called you out of darkness into His marvelous light (1 Peter 2:9).

What happens in life when all the ingredients for a beautiful rainbow are present, but there is no rainbow in sight? One particular summer, I would have given anything to have seen one. Yes, the sun may have been shining outside, but inside the Logan, it was stormy. (And no relief was in sight.)

When one of our managers asked if we would allow her to bring a friend to the Logan for the summer, we thought it would be okay. The agreement was that she would live with us, work elsewhere, and help us out whenever she could.

As the summer wore on, I felt like we had made a terrible mistake. Jackie seemed to be so miserable around us. Nothing I did seemed to make the situation any better. I remember a certain wicker chair on the porch where she would sit when she was out of sorts (which was most of the time). The scowl on her face seemed to be an indication of what was brewing in her hurting heart. We thought it would have made her happy to be with her friend for the summer and have free room and board. She must have thought we meant "bored." On very rare occasions, a momentary smile would slip out. During those times, I thought I caught a glimpse of hidden sweetness. Other than that, we had nothing else to hold on to.

"Oh Father, please bring Jackie to Yourself. Help us to look past the glares and love her," I'd pray desperately. But we never saw any changes. Those glares kept us all at a distance.

"Larry, do you think we made a mistake by letting her come? Maybe we didn't pray about it enough," I lamented.

"Joyce, God is faithful," he reminded me. "He will work it for good somehow. The summer is already half over. God will help us to get through."

"Okay," I muttered. Then grasping at a thread of hope I said, "Maybe we are planting some seeds of God's love in her life. That's the only thing that keeps me going."

It was a very long summer. Many afternoons when the girls went to the beach, I would go out to the front porch, sit in Jackie's chair, and pray: "God, please complete the work You have started in her" (see Phil. 1:6).

We are always glad when the season comes to an end so that we can breathe a sigh of relief. This time, I think the sigh was loud enough to be heard in Somer's Point (a place across the bay)!

The girls packed up their things and prepared to drive back to Maryland. I hugged and thanked each girl as I said, "Good-bye."

"Good-bye, Jackie," I said as she climbed into her car. Mixed emotions came to the surface of my heart as I watched her drive out of sight. It was a mixture of relief and sorrow. I remember tears filling my eyes over this person whom I would probably never see again. The storm clouds lifted, and somehow the Logan seemed a little brighter.

Many years later we received an unexpected Christmas card. It was the "rainbow" that we had been waiting for! It read something like this:

> "Dear Larry and Joyce, I thought that you, of all people, would like to know that I became born again. Thanks for putting up with me that summer at the Logan. I was going through a very hard time in my life. I'm sorry for all the trouble that I caused you. Love in Christ, Jackie."

We were so happy to write back to her, but then we lost touch once more.

Years later, Larry and I went to a local pregnancy center's fund-raising banquet. After finding our table, I went into the hall to find the ladies' room. (Those of you with "birdie bladders" will understand.) Rather than wandering around, I decided to ask for directions at the information desk. The woman whom I talked to called a young lady over to direct me. I thought it was so nice that she was willing to show me the way. After a few moments, we turned to look at each other. Her smile was strangely familiar. It took a couple of seconds for us to realize what was happening. "Jackie?" I gasped. "Joyce?" she said in response. Imagine that! The Lord used my birdie bladder, of all things, to bring us face to face right there in the hallway. People must have thought we were long lost friends the way we laughed and cried and hugged one another. And actually, we really were!

"I can't believe it!" she exclaimed.

"After all these years, God brought us together again!" I said, embracing this very huggable young woman and loving every minute of it. "You are so beautiful!" I said as I basked in the miracle-working power of the Lord. We exchanged phone numbers with the promise of getting together soon to catch up. I couldn't wait to go back to the table to tell Larry about what God had done on the way to the ladies' room!

Several days later, we met for lunch and Jackie told me the incredible story of how God had changed her life. She had been working for a very liberal organization when God apprehended her with His love. Now, her heart's desire was to serve Him full time at pregnancy centers in the area. As she talked, her smile, her countenance, and her love for Jesus overwhelmed me. I didn't want to take my eyes off her. I must have smiled all the way home. God "is able to do exceeding abundantly beyond all that we ask or think" (Eph. 3:20).

I quietly praised God, "Lord, You've done it again! You transformed Jackie's life and brought her back to us so we could see it with our own eyes. You knew her potential all along! It was worth all the heartache. After all, if we hadn't known the old Jackie, we wouldn't have been able to appreciate the new one. It reminds me of going through labor pains. It's worth it all just to hold a miracle in your arms!"

"Father God, in Your Word You tell us not to judge anything before the time (see 1 Cor. 4:5). Forgive us for judging others by what we see. Please train our eyes to see the potential of the human heart. Thank You for the thrill of holding miracles in our arms—in Jesus' name we pray, amen."

But God demonstrates His own love toward us, in that while we were yet sinners, Christ died for us (Romans 5:8).

Memories From the Attic

Some of my fondest memories of the Logan include waking up in the middle of a severe thunderstorm and going downstairs to sit on the porch in the early morning hours to watch the rain and feel the mist on my face and looking at the sea, getting a visual image of the Scripture: "The seas have lifted up, O Lord, the seas have lifted up their voice; the seas have lifted up their pounding waves. Mightier than the thunder of the great waters, mightier than the breakers of the sea–the Lord on high is mighty" (Ps. 93:3-4 NIV). My very first time at the Logan was on a church retreat as a young girl of eight or nine. I remember sitting in the picnic table area, looking up at the hotel, and wondering what all those rooms looked like inside, what was behind all the closed doors, and what it was like to be one of those girls who got to clean the rooms. Little did I know then that the Lord would grant me years of that very experience. I remember my love for hanging out the clean sheets on the clotheslines outside and the one time that we checked people into a room before it was cleaned. I remember the picture in the living room of the boy and wagon and the horse being shod; how good the ice cold water from the porch fountain tasted after a hard morning of cleaning; organizing the linen closets; picking the verses to grace the top of our checklist for the next day; baking disaster cookies with Kristen (in which we forgot to add the white sugar and the only way they could be eaten was underneath piles of ice cream); and the bold seagulls who expertly swoop away with prizes from unsuspecting persons on the boardwalk. Yet these are just a few of my favorite things.

Patricia Rice '90-'98

Each and every morning, we would all start the day at 7:00 a.m. with Bible study. I have never been a morning person, so this was the greatest challenge for me. I would have to practically use toothpicks to pry open my eyes each morning. My Mom would often awake us to the familiar tune, "This is the Day the Lord has Made." She would sing this in her most joyful voice. I would lay in my bed and wonder how God could make anyone quite this "chipper" at such an early hour of the day. I love my Mom!

Even though I complained about having to get up for Bible study every morning, this set the stage for my Christian growth. I learned many good lessons each summer, including what it means to be a godly woman. I am still continuing to learn about Him. Through chambermaiding and managing at the Logan, I learned how to relate to people, manage money and time, and how to do about ten things at once. I also found that my quiet times on the beach were some of the times when I have felt the closest to God. I love looking out at the ocean and taking in the awesomeness of God's creation. He still reminds me often of the verse that says, "Be still, and know that I am God" (Ps. 46:10a KJV). How quickly we forget this in the busyness of our lives.

Kristi (Coffin) Ivosevich '73-'85

Chapter 12

Disturbing the Peace?

Shout joyfully to the Lord, all the earth. Serve the Lord with gladness; come before Him with joyful singing. Know that the Lord Himself is God; it is He who has made us, and not we ourselves; we are His people and the sheep of His pasture. Enter His gates with thanksgiving, and His courts with praise. Give thanks to Him; bless His name. For the Lord is good; His lovingkindness is everlasting, and His faithfulness to all generations (Psalm 100).

For as long as I can remember, we have had a Saturday night sing-along on the front porch of the Logan. Each time is unique. We have different combinations of voices from the gathering of staff, guests, and Christians in the neighborhood. Sometimes people passing by the hotel come up from the sidewalk and ask to join us. We sing a variety of hymns and praise songs on request. Occasionally, we've been known to have guitars, violins, flutes, and even Conga drums. Sometimes people call for reservations at the Logan because they have heard us singing in the past. One man said he had even joined us from his bed in a nearby guesthouse.

Usually halfway through the singing, we all introduce ourselves and tell where we are from and what we do.

Praise reports are also shared at this time. (Even the little children participate.) These sing-alongs are always such a blessing that many of our former guests arrange their reservations so they can be with us for Saturday night.

One evening while we were singing praises to the Lord, two policemen came up on the porch. They told us that someone had called in a complaint that we were disturbing the peace. They looked so embarrassed when they realized what we were doing. (As a result we start the sing-along at eight o'clock instead of nine now.) We found out later that there was a wild party a couple of houses down from the Logan. We figured that they had the wrong house. Maybe there was a reason God brought them to the sing-along that night...Time will tell!

One Saturday night, a guest was late getting back for the singing. As the woman came down Sixth Street, she noticed an unmistakable glow coming from the hotel. "The Logan looks like a *lighthouse*," she exclaimed. Looking back, I remember that the presence of the Lord had been very strong that night as we worshiped God. I pray that His light will continue to shine through all we say and sing and do, even when we are falsely accused.

"Lord Jesus, we honor You as our Prince of Peace. You know more than anyone what it is like to be falsely accused. You always respond in love. Help us to respect authority, even when we disagree. You never ask us to do anything that You don't enable us to do. As we yield to Your authority in our lives, may we be beacons of light to draw others (even police officers) into the saving knowledge of Your grace. In Jesus' name we pray, amen."

Memories From the Attic

Working at the Logan was always an interesting experience. It was a wonderful way to get to know the other girls. We were paired up to work and had a chart where we were to sign up for whatever job was open. On the chart, you would find listed "showers, public bathrooms (we called them 'pb's', room changeovers, make beds, water flowers, etc." Often we would have various interesting and crazy situations either with the guests or the vacuums or maybe even with the washing machines and dryers!

Lunch was always laid-back, and it was a good time to talk and decide what fun things we were going to do that afternoon. My favorite thing to do was go to the beach and spend the day tanning in the warm sun and swimming in the all-too-often freezing water. I also enjoyed shopping on rainy days. When I first began working at the Logan, I really enjoyed walking the boardwalk and spending money on frivolous things. I was fascinated by all the stores and the different fun possibilities on the boardwalk, such as miniature golf and eating Mack & Mancos pizza–an Ocean City, New Jersey, favorite.

Other responsibilities at the hotel included helping out with the laundry, making dinner (for staff and sometimes visitors), and cleaning the public bathrooms again in the evening. Each of these jobs truly helped me learn how to be a responsible and hardworking woman.

Jenny Parent '91-'99

Chapter 13

"Come Unto Me"

There remains therefore a Sabbath rest for the people of God (Hebrews 4:9).

Many people had asked us for a business card for the hotel. We didn't have one.

Larry and I were discussing possibilities as we sat at the breakfast table one morning when one of our chambermaids came in. "Come sit down, Sue. We're trying to think of a good verse to put on the back of the business card," Larry said, as he leafed through his Bible.

Without pausing for a moment, Sue said, "Come to Me, all who are weary and heavy-laden, and I will give you rest" (Mt. 11:28). It was as if the Lord had spoken through her!

"That's it!" Larry said with excitement. It was perfect! And we all knew it.

Sue looked shocked. "I didn't even think about it," Sue exclaimed. "I opened my mouth, and it just came out!"

We all sat amazed. We knew it couldn't have been more perfect. Jehovah-Jireh, our Provider, had moved again on our behalf, showing us the desire of His heart. We bask in the wonder of it even today.

Sometimes when I feel anything but peaceful, the Lord reminds me of that verse in Matthew, and I too am able to find the rest I need. I picture myself on His lap with my head on His breast. His presence reassures and comforts me time and time again. Sometimes I pour my heart out to Him. Sometimes I'm too weary to even do anything but weep. He holds me in His arms of love until I am able to sleep. What a wonderful, loving God we have!

Many weary travelers have sensed His presence here and have found rest for their bodies and souls.

The secret to this rest is not coming to the Logan. The secret is coming to Jesus! We can't help but love Him once we come to know Him. In the light of His unconditional love and acceptance (He receives us just as we are), we find the peace and rest that we so desperately need.

The business card still sits on the front desk of the Logan. It's a constant reminder of His beckoning call to one and all: "Come unto Me!"

"Dear gentle Jesus, like weary, weather-beaten ships on a storm-tossed sea, we come to Thee. We entrust our heavy-laden hearts into Your holy, healing hands. You draw us close and whisper, 'Stay,' even when we are too tired to pray. We come looking forward to the "rest" of our lives with You! In Jesus' name we pray, amen."

Surely I have composed and quieted my soul; like a weaned child rests against his mother, my soul is like a weaned child within me (Psalm 131:2).

And you shall find rest for your souls (Matthew 11:29b).

Memories From the Attic

I have some great memories of going to Bible school at the local Presbyterian church; taking tennis lessons across the street from Robbie; making new friends; participating in basketball and gymnastics camps; biking on the boards; playing hide-and-go-seek in the lockers out back with my brother; and watching awesome fireworks from the second-story rooftop on the Fourth of July. I enjoyed the early morning hunts for starfish with my grandmother and swimming with her "way out" in the deep part of the ocean. We used to go out as far as we could–until the lifeguard summoned us in with his whistle.

I learned to cook at the age of two, and I have been perfecting my cooking over the past 32 years. The girls who worked at the Logan would all take turns cooking various meals each night. This way, my Mom could be relieved from having this duty every day. The scary part of this was the fact that many of the girls had never set foot in a kitchen before, let alone be able to distinguish a spatula from a rolling pin. We ate many mystery meals over those years. Some meals we were eventually able to identify, and others remain a mystery to this day.

Kristi (Coffin) Ivosevich '73-'85

Chapter 14

Like a Mighty Wind

He will cover you with His pinions, and under His wings you may seek refuge; His faithfulness is a shield and bulwark (Psalm 91:4).

A hurricane was heading up the eastern seaboard. The guests paced back and forth in the lobby with their eyes glued to the weather channel. As time went on, it became evident that the Jersey coast would experience some of the hurricane's fury.

We had no idea how long the storm would have us housebound, so we stocked up on staples at the grocery store. If it was as bad as the forecasters predicted, we would be feeding not only the staff but also the guests who decided to brave the storm as well.

I was so busy with canceling reservations that I neglected to have my quiet time. Toward the end of the morning, I felt compelled by the Holy Spirit to go to the beach to write His message in the sand. "What would You like me to write?" I asked the Lord. Without a moment's hesitation, it came to me: "Who is this man, that even the winds and waves obey Him?" (Lk. 8:25b TLB)

I ran down to the beach to complete the task before the tide came in. Many people had gathered on the boardwalk to watch as the waves grew in size and intensity. It looked as though the Lord had taken a giant eggbeater and whipped up the waves for as far as the eye could see. The air was charged with excitement!

The wind was blowing so hard that I had trouble keeping my balance as I wrote the six-foot letters in the hardened sand. Pushing past the embarrassment, I focused on the work God had given me to do. I knew that God's message was more important than what people might think of me. Perhaps it would be used for eternal purposes! I got more excited as time went on. I knew that His Word goes out of His mouth and doesn't return to Him empty (see Is. 55:11). That promise spurred me on. I realized that people are usually more receptive during times like these. Completing the task, I picked up my shoes and headed back to the Logan, turning one last time to take a look at those waves. "Even the winds and waves obey You, Lord," I repeated, reflecting on the verse that I had just written on the sand and marveling at His awesome power.

Meanwhile, back at the Logan, Mom had already started to prepare a big pot of spaghetti sauce. The chambermaids were getting a head start on the salad that was being made in the dishpan. (It was the biggest thing that they could find.) If no one else checked out, I calculated that we would have 28 for the evening meal. A big supply of bread and peanut butter and jelly was in the cupboard. We collected every available container and filled it with water. The bathtubs were filled as well. The chairs on the front porch were stacked, and the trashcans were placed in the showers in the rear of the building so that they wouldn't blow away. We made sure that the locker doors were closed and the bathing suits and beach towels were brought in off the clotheslines out back.

About 3:00 p.m., the storm had so increased in its intensity that we were experiencing high winds and driving rains. Larry called everyone into the lobby. He read Psalm 91. Twenty-eight of us joined hands and prayed for God's protection. It's amazing how close you feel to others when you're huddled together under His wings.

You probably are wondering why we didn't leave. (At times, I wondered that myself!) I prayed for wisdom for Larry, the head of our household, and he felt that we should stay put. The emergency center for Ocean City was in the high school right across the street. We were on high ground as well. Trying to get off the island at that point would have been dangerous. Cars were bumper to bumper on the causeway. Waves were already licking at the tires. Even after getting onto the mainland, there were a lot of low-lying areas between Somer's Point and I-95. Larry had made the right decision to stay.

The hurricane raged outside! The water in the street came up within an inch of going into the ground-level apartments, but we stayed dry, warm, and unshaken. (That is, unless you tried to lie on one of the beds. The wind blew against the building so hard that they felt like vibrator beds hooked up to some big machine...for which we didn't charge any extra.)

One of the most fun things to do was run up to the attic and watch the raging sea out the windows from five stories up! (We had to go up there periodically anyway to make sure the coffee cans were in the right places to catch the leaks.)

By midnight, the worst was over and we could sleep soundly.

The next day was beautiful! The deep blue sky was so clear. It was as though the clouds had been wiped out by a giant eraser. The air was fresh and clean. Had the hurricane been only a figment of our imagination? (The debris along the shoreline and hearing about the extensive damage to neighboring Atlantic City brought us back to reality.)

I became aware of the fact that even when we are not experiencing storms, the mighty wind of the Spirit blows through the Logan. Waves of His presence continue to wash over us as we endeavor to do His will. This was confirmed as two of the couples checked out the next day.

One of the men came up to me with tears in his eyes. Holding both of my hands, he leaned over the desk, looked me right in the eye, and said, "Joyce, I just want you to know what a blessing it has been for us to be here at the 'LIGHTHOUSE,' during the storm."

My mouth flew open. He had no way of knowing what God had laid on my heart! It was amazing to me that someone else also knew that the Logan was His Lighthouse.

"Lord we stand in awe of Your mighty power. We feel so vulnerable and weak when the storms of life wreak havoc around us. It's comforting to know that all the winds and waves obcy You, Jesus. May Your light so shine through us that those who are lost will also find their way into the shelter of Your wings. In Jesus' name we pray, amen."

Memories From the Attic

The first memories I have of the Logan are of the attic, which are, in my opinion, the most delicious of coveted living quarters in all Ocean City. The attic has a view from each end of the house. It has winds from each end too. Some mornings I would awake to pigeons or the sounds of cooing doves. (There was that one occasion when the bird came indoors for a more direct wake-up call!) It was not a resort; it was a simple place that a handful of girls called their bedroom each summer.

Although the attic has its own aura, it is incomplete without the girls. I remember staying up there one September without any other ladies. The first hour was beautiful in silence. But after that, the silence left room for other noises or for what felt simply like a dull void in my heart. A summer night was not complete unless I had to tell the girls to "quiet down" after 11:00 p.m., or declare, "Lights out!"

For those who were pre-college, the attic was a taste of dorm life–shared facilities, courteousness to others who were sleeping, and of course, shared clothing. And with the boardwalk only one block away, life consisted of praying, working, eating, beaching, and boardwalking.

Emily McDermitt '87-'98

Chapter 15

A Scream in the Night

You will not be afraid of the terror by night... (Psalm 91:5).

He was tall, dark, and handsome, but something about his presence unnerved me. Far in the distance, I could hear a bloodcurdling scream. As I came up through multiple levels of consciousness, I became aware that my own mouth was wide open. The scream was coming from me! (I didn't know that I could scream like that!) It sounded like something from a horror movie!

Putting his arms around me, Larry tried to calm me down. I was so traumatized that my first reaction was to push him away. Finally, I was able to rest in the comfort of his arms.

"It must have been a bad dream," I told him. (But I never remember my dreams.) *There must be a deeper meaning*, I thought.

The next day I had to deal with the embarrassing repercussions.

As people came down the steps in the morning I asked, "Did you have a good night?" (I was almost afraid to hear the answer.) If they said, "Yes," I breathed a sigh of relief. If they said, "No," I cringed.

One of the guests announced to a lobby full of people, "There must have been a mugging in the alley last night!" I was speechless. Others chimed in saying, "We heard that scream in the night as well." Finally, I admitted that I had heard it too, but I didn't elaborate.

"Lord, this is all so mystifying, but You must have allowed the dream for a reason. Is there something that You want me to learn from this?" I prayed silently.

As I was eating breakfast with some of my family members, of course the subject came up. (Poor Larry was still recuperating from the shock of it all.) I began to describe the episode to them. Without missing a heartbeat, one of my relatives said, "The devil made you do it." I thought that he was just trying to make light of it. Then he looked me straight in the eye and said, very sternly, "I'm telling you–it was satan!"

Well, he had never said anything like that before! He was so serious by now, that I didn't know what to make of it. The man in my dream had been so nice-looking, but I did remember reading in Second Corinthians 11:14 that even "Satan disguises himself as an angel of light."

The day before all this happened, I had been reading one of Catherine Marshall's books, *Something More*. Leaving it open to mark my place, I turned it over and put it on the little windowsill between the kitchen and the first-floor hall where it had laid all night.

After breakfast, I felt compelled to pick up the book. Oddly enough, the pages had been turned to the next chapter. It was called "The Fallen Angel." My eyes fell on a portion of the text that described a woman's dream. She was in bed and opened her eyes to see a tall, dark man standing at the foot of her bed. His presence terrified her. Immediately, the Good Shepherd appeared beside her with a staff in His hand. He said, "...everything that the devil and man can do to you are not going to harm you as long as you stay close to Me. Don't ever again let any of his life live in you or have any power over you."[1] Then as the woman thought of the changes God had brought about in her life, the "personification of evil" left.

I don't believe in coincidences. That message had to be for me! As I sought the Lord, He revealed cracks in my armor where the enemy had gotten in and built landing strips.

I confessed areas of pride and fear that I had been entertaining for years. I love that Scripture in Acts 3:19 that says, "Repent therefore and return, that your sins may be wiped away, in order that times of refreshing may come from the presence of the Lord." There was such a stark contrast between God's presence (which brought the joy of repentance) and the presence of the fallen angel (which brought fear, terror, and condemnation). Even though hard things still happen in my life, there is a peace in knowing that the Good Shepherd is protecting me in the midst of it all. When the enemy attacks after those landing strips are closed and put out of commission, I at least know it's not because I have given him permission.

I've never had that dream again!

"Dear Lord, as the Shepherd and the Guardian of our souls, You laid down Your life for Your sheep. We should fear no evil if we stay close to You. Reveal cracks in our armor where the enemy has built landing strips. Thank You for the blood of Jesus that cleanses and protects us even when we are asleep—in Jesus' name we pray, amen."

1. Catherine Marshall, *Something More* (Grand Rapids, MI: Chosen Books, a division of Baker Book House, 1974), 121-122.

You are from God, little children, and have overcome them; because greater is He who is in you than he who is in the world (1 John 4:4).

Memories From the Attic

One important and necessary lesson I learned at the Logan is the importance of memorizing Scripture. I recall earning many small prizes, but the summer of my senior year in high school I had my eyes fixed on a certain hot pink insulated lunch pack with a purple strap.

At the time I was very disheartened because in order to win that particular prize I would have to memorize, not just one or two verses of Scripture, but an entire chapter! I really wanted that lunch pack though, so I began my quest and told Joyce of my plans. She suggested that I look in the Book of Psalms. As I searched the Scripture in my NIV Student Bible, I came across a chapter that was not only short enough to memorize, but I also truly loved the words–Psalm 46! I started to find time to sneak away up to the attic where I would meditate on and memorize the psalm. I knew that the hot pink insulated lunch pack would soon be mine! What I did not know, though, was that the Lord would later give me something that would stay in my heart forever.

Well, that summer quickly passed, and it was soon my last week at the Logan. I was preparing to go to college in a couple of weeks, and my heart and my head were burdened with thoughts of what was to happen when I was finally on my own for the first time in my life. One day during that last week, I was especially anxious. It was overcast and cool, so I decided to clear my head by going for a walk. I ended up in the empty basketball court across the street. The court was filled with puddles from the previous night's rain, and as I stood on the quiet court looking at the Logan, the Lord's presence filled my heart, and I heard, "Sarah, be still and know that I am God" (see Ps. 46:10 NIV). I was immediately filled with the peace that passes all understanding (see Phil. 4:7). A burden had been lifted, my heart was at rest, and I had been given my first ***rhema*** *(a special saying the Lord had given just to me)! I quickly went back to the Logan to tell everyone what had happened, and I opened my Bible and wrote next to Psalm 46:10, "summer of 1993."*

Although I am married now and live near a different beach, whenever I get anxious I still feel God tapping at my heart telling me to be still, cease striving, and just trust in Him. Sometimes I pull out the Student Bible that I used that summer and look at the verse as a reminder of God's faithfulness and of the peace that only He can give. As for the hot pink insulated lunch pack with the purple strap, it has a small tear on the top and sits in the cupboard waiting for my next treasured visit to the beach.

Sarah (Fowler) Towles '90-'93

Chapter 16

"Behold the Lamb!"

Behold the Lamb of God, which taketh away the sin of the world (John 1:29b KJV).

The word *behold* has fascinated me for years. "Lord, teach me what it means to behold You," I'd pray on many occasions. The insight came in three different ways—through my husband, through the Song of Solomon, and through John the Baptist.

Larry and I are so busy at the Logan from Memorial Day to the week after Labor Day that we don't always have quality time with each other. We rush past one another in the hall and maybe give one another a little love pat from time to time, but it's far from "beholding." When we do take a moment to sit down on the porch or in the lobby, we generally end up talking to others. Our windows of opportunity are usually closed before we have a chance to take advantage of them. We love being with our guests and our staff, but somehow time for each other gets put on the back burner.

I believe that the Lord uses things in the natural to teach us things of the Spirit. Marriage is supposed to represent

Jesus and His relationship with His Bride (the Church). Therefore, it's obvious to me why the enemy is doing his level best to destroy "the evidence."

Similarly, quality time with the Lord is often difficult to come by. Usually, prayer time is interrupted by well-meaning knocks on my door. As I started to contemplate the word *behold* I found this verse in Song of Solomon 4:1: "How beautiful you are, my darling, how beautiful you are! Your eyes are like doves behind your veil...." Further study revealed that a dove has no peripheral vision. It can only look straight ahead. "What I need are dove's eyes!" I said out loud. "Lord, I really want to behold You with 'undistracted devotion' " (see 1 Cor. 7:35). The problem is that no one despises dove's eyes like the father of lies, so it takes a concerted effort to behold the Lamb in the manner that He deserves. And without those dove's eyes there is no other way to give Jesus that kind of undivided attention. In time, I've come to believe that to behold Him I must take time to adore Him, to appreciate His attributes, to worship Him for who He is (not for what I can get from Him), to whisper words of love in His ear, to sing love songs to Him, to seek His face, and to tell Him how much He means to me. Prayerful love pats are fine, but nothing takes the place of beholding!

More than ever, I see the importance of putting on "dove's eyes" in order to behold the two most important people in my life. Once I get my priorities in order, everything else will fall into place.

Have you ever thought about what an awesome privilege it is to "behold the Lamb"? Just try to imagine the sights and sounds beyond the Jordan River as we look in on one of the servants of the Lord.

Can't you just hear the voice of John the Baptist crying in the wilderness, "...Make straight the way of the Lord..." (Jn. 1:23)? Can't you just see him humbly baptizing the multitudes, knowing all along that he was just a forerunner? He knew that the One who was coming after him would be so great that he wouldn't even feel worthy to untie His sandals (see Jn. 1:27). Wouldn't you have loved to have been there on that day of days when he lifted his eyes and saw Jesus coming through the crowds? Then, in a voice that still echos down through the ages, he boldly proclaimed, "Behold, the Lamb of God who takes away the sin of the world!" (Jn. 1:29b) On that very day, John was given the awesome privilege of baptizing the Lamb!

The Jews had celebrated the annual Feast of Passover ever since they had left Egypt. Every year they had to kill an unblemished male lamb at twilight and roast it with fire. They were instructed to eat it with unleavened bread and bitter herbs. In the original Passover, the blood of the lamb had to be applied to the doorpost and lintel of their houses to protect them from the coming judgment.

> *And the blood shall be a sign for you on the houses where you live; and when I see the blood I will pass over you, and no plague will befall you to destroy you when I strike the land of Egypt. Now this day will be a memorial to you, and you shall celebrate it as a feast to the Lord; throughout your generations you are to celebrate it as a permanent ordinance* (Exodus 12:13-14).

When God inaugurated the Passover, He was setting the stage for an event that would take place about 1,400 years later!

The time had finally arrived for the "ultimate" Passover Lamb to come onto the scene. Through the sacrifice of His blood (placed on the doorposts and lintels of yielded hearts), He would atone for the sin of the whole world. There would be no more need for sacrifices, once God's unblemished Lamb was slain. The need for atonement would be satisfied once and for all on the cross when Jesus cried out with a voice that echos throughout eternity, "It is finished!" (Jn. 19:30) This plan of atonement was in the Father's heart from the beginning of time (see Rev. 13:8).

> *For God so loved the world, that He gave His only begotten Son, that whoever believes in Him should not perish, but have eternal life* (John 3:16).

Oh, what a lavish gift of love from God the Father! He loved this unworthy world so much that He sent His only Son to be the sacrificial Lamb!

Can't you just imagine the look on John's face as Jesus came up out of the water and he beheld the Spirit descending as a dove out of Heaven and remaining upon Him (see Jn. 1:32)?

Have you ever thought about the crowd of people who witnessed what happened that day? I wonder how many realized what was actually taking place. Were they busy talking to one another, or was there a dead silence as they stood at the water's edge? Is it possible that they too could have "beheld the Lamb" but missed the opportunity for one reason or another? Perhaps they were not spiritually in tune or were not really hungry for something more in their lives. Maybe they were plagued with doubts and fears. Some came so close to beholding the Lamb only to have missed the blessing in their midst because they failed to recognize Him.

I was surprised to see that John the Baptist didn't recognize Jesus at first either—not until the Father opened his eyes. The Scripture says in John 1:33-34,

> *And I did not recognize Him, but He who sent me to baptize in water said to me, "He upon whom you see the Spirit descending and remaining upon Him, this is the one*

who baptizes in the Holy Spirit. And I have seen, and have borne witness that this is the Son of God."

Even though we are a Christian hotel, we welcome anyone who comes through the door (as long as they agree to the rules). A Jewish man by the name of David came to stay at the Logan. One day, a group of us were sitting in the lobby and the subject came up about Jesus. I seized the opportunity and said, "You know, David, some Jews actually believe that Jesus is the Messiah." He looked indignant and replied, "If that's the case, they are no longer Jews!"

If I had tried to think of an answer on my own, it wouldn't have been nearly as convincing as the one I feel the Lord gave to me at that moment:

"David, do you believe that the Messiah will come someday?" I asked.

"Yes, I do!" he said without batting an eye.

"Well, when He comes, and you believe that He has come, does that mean you are no longer a Jew?" There was dead silence. He quietly walked out of the lobby. Either he was afraid to consider that the Messiah had already come or he, like so many others, was blinded by the father of lies. I continue to pray for the Lord to open David's eyes so that he too will "see and bear witness that Jesus is the Son of God" (see Jn. 1:34).

"Dear heavenly Father, we stand in awe at the unfolding of Your plan for the Lamb. Open the eyes of our understanding so that we can recognize Him and not miss the blessing in our midst. How we long to behold Him with undistracted devotion, looking forward to the day He will say, 'You are beautiful, My darling; your eyes are like dove's behind your veil'—in Jesus' name we pray, amen."

Memories From the Attic

My experiences at the Logan really shaped me as a person. Two summers ago, at the age of 17, I became a Logan manager, and my responsibilities increased greatly. In addition to chambermaiding, I also got to work behind the desk taking calls, making reservations, and checking guests in. I remember that when I went through training, I was incredibly nervous. There was much information and very little time to learn it. Eventually, though, everything came to me as if it were second nature.

At the Logan, we had some special rules that I knew most places didn't have. For instance, we didn't allow unmarried couples to stay with us. We asked that there would be no drinking or smoking and we had quiet hours between 10:00 p.m. and 9:00 a.m. The hotel was really geared toward families and older couples. When I began working as a manager, I was warned that I would be faced with some extremely difficult situations. However, I didn't expect to face these situations on my very first shift ever. My first phone call was for a church group retreat that needed a lot of rooms. Talk about overwhelming! I had to turn away an unmarried couple in my very second phone call. Still, I was glad to get the experience out of the way so that I knew how to better handle it the next time I was faced with it.

Managing gave me the feeling that somehow I was an owner of the Logan, not just an employee. I had a big responsibility, and I knew that the way I presented myself to each and every guest who walked through the door would make an impact on their lives and make an impression on them as to what the Logan was like. As my bosses always told me, "You're the first person our guests will see when they walk through that front door." That always reminded me to have a smile on my face, and a patient and willing attitude.

Over the course of the seven summers that I worked at the hotel, the Logan truly became my second home, so much so that I became "homesick" somewhere around January of each school year, longing for the summer and for the chance I would have to get back to the shore and to all my friends at the hotel.

Friends! Oh, how many wonderful friends I made while at the Logan! I am happy to say that I made lifelong friends with my co-workers and even among some of the guests. What a blessing!

The Logan helped shape me into the person that I am today. My spiritual life has been enhanced. I've learned a lot of useful and practical things, and I've made fun and godly friends. Being a chambermaid and a manager at the Logan hotel is an experience that I will never forget.

Jenny Parent '91-'99

Chapter 17

Pecking Order

And be kind to one another, tender-hearted, forgiving each other, just as God in Christ also has forgiven you (Ephesians 4:32).

I never expected to learn a lesson in marriage as I went down to the beach that morning. It looked as though the seagulls had gathered for a convention. Have you ever wondered how they get the word out? God's creatures are so amazing!

In the midst of the tumult, two of the gulls had taken center stage. I watched as the female screeched at what seemed to be her mate. He fluttered his feathers and jumped backwards with each screech. After several altercations and many attempts on his part to be reconciled, it became more than he could handle. He took flight, never to return again. The female wandered around, looking bewildered, as if she didn't have a clue.

As I watched this little drama unfold, I was profoundly impacted by the following words of wisdom: "*Humility* is always the first one to say, 'I'm sorry.' *Pride* always thinks it has to have the last word."

"Lord, convict us when we start to henpeck our hubbies. Please give us fresh, new ways to bless their hearts instead. After all, as we serve them, we are, in reality, serving You. May we respond to them in such a way that they will always enjoy being in our company. In Jesus' name we pray, amen."

Memories From the Attic

The Logan hotel–a welcoming yearly vacation spot for some, a friendly weekend getaway for others, but for me, coming to the Logan is like coming home. Two things you can always count on when you work at the Logan are hugs from Joyce and Larry and "go around the table" for dinnertime conversation.

How do I even begin to express the ways that working at the Logan has touched and impacted my life? I remember waking every morning to see an orange-and-blue-streaked sky and a dolphin-blue ocean. There are so many things that come to mind when I think of the Logan, but one of my fondest memories is of a valuable lesson I learned during my first summer.

It was a normal morning of making beds, cleaning rooms, washing and drying laundry, and racing to answer ringing phones as I mumbled a quick "excuse me" to an innocent guest who happened to be in my path. I was racing from room to room and making what seemed like my hundredth trip up the first of five flights of stairs when I heard Joyce's cheerful voice call, "Shannon, where are you going with that fan?" I suppose that it was at that particular moment, with sweat beading on my forehead and my sweaty palms clutching the fan, that the question struck me as unnecessary, and I snapped, "To Room 21, Joyce!" It was not my words that came out disrespectfully, but the impatient tone I had used. I waited for the rebuke to come, but Joyce simply asked me if I could change my course and take the fan to Room 14 instead. "Yes," I replied, and I continued up the stairs...somehow that fan had gained about 20 pounds.

The conversation had taken only a few short seconds, but it hung in my mind throughout the rest of the morning. I suspected that I was in for a "Room 5 Talk," and we all knew what that meant–me and Joyce conferring in her room–alone! That was enough to make me dread the experience. It wasn't that I was afraid of being yelled at. I have never heard Joyce raise her voice to anyone, but coming from a family where yelling was sometimes our format for discussion, the silence and quietness I encountered when I entered the room was worse than 1,000 voices shouting at once.

But it was during that quiet conversation in Room 5 that I began to understand the importance of respectfully responding to authority.

I also began to learn the unspoken lesson of discipline administered in love. God worked in my life in special ways that summer, beginning with that quiet "Room 5 Talk." Today, I am a high school English teacher, and these are the lessons I desire for my students to learn and the lesson I still require of myself.

The Logan hotel–a vacation spot for some, a friendly weekend getaway for others, but for me it's like coming home....

Shannon Snow '97-'98

Chapter 18

A Basket of Trouble

Therefore, behold, I will allure her, bring her into the wilderness, and speak kindly to her. Then I will give her her vineyards from there, and the valley of Achor [Trouble] as a door of hope (Hosea 2:14-15a).

One of the most horrible times in my life was during the summer and fall of 1990. The Logan furnace was spewing black oil on the properties around us; Mom was diagnosed with inoperable lung cancer; the enemy was attacking the unity of my family; and I was experiencing some dizziness that seemed to stem from it all. During this horrendous time, my mind flashed back to several years before when I was Christmas shopping. We bought gifts for a lot of families in those days. Money was scarce, so I became a bargain shopper. The word went out that a store in town had the "Trouble" game on sale for $1.99! This was a bargain that was too good to pass up! First thing in the morning, I got up and ran to be first in line when the doors opened. Trying not to bump into the other early birds, I made my way into the store. I grabbed the first cart in sight and headed down the game aisle.

Relieved to see that there were several "Trouble" games still left on the shelf, I proceeded to stack the boxes on top of each other in the basket of my cart. Picture the scene: "TROUBLE" was printed on every side of each box in large letters. The stack was so high that I had to steady it with one hand while pushing the cart with the other. Needless to say, this drew a lot of attention as I maneuvered the cart toward the checkout counter.

"Boy, lady, do you have trouble!" "Look at all the trouble that lady has!" and "She's really asking for trouble if you ask me!" were only some of the comments that were made that day. I just smiled, knowing that it must have been a pretty funny sight. It reminds me of the reactions I get when I pile my cart full of toilet paper at the Super Fresh in Ocean City. (The people there don't usually comment but I still get some funny looks!)

Now, during that summer of 1990, the girls and I had been studying the Hebrew names of God in Kay Arthur's book, *Lord, I Want to Know You.* It's an excellent study. The Hebrew name for the Most High God is *El Elyon*, the sovereign God. (This is important to the story.) When my mind flashed back to that basket full of "Trouble," it was as if the Lord said, "No matter how high your troubles stack, I am higher still. I am the Most High God!"

I desperately clung to His words like a life preserver during that difficult time. When so many things in my life were out of control, I knew that El Elyon, the Most High God, was still in control.

He was in control as the furnace spewed black pieces of carbon paper particles all over the neighbor's laundry on the clotheslines and over the grassy carpeting on the surrounding patios. The little carbon-like pieces became oil upon contact! I had to use an old vacuum cleaner and crawl around on my hands and knees, holding the nozzle up six inches from the ground to suck them up before they liquified. (The Scripture that came to mind as I cried tears of frustration was, "He gives me beauty for ashes, the oil of joy for mourning, the garment of praise for the spirit of heaviness" [see Is. 61:3 KJV].)

We called the chimney sweep. After he finished cleaning out the system, he turned the boiler back on, and it was even worse! We tried squirting the oil off of the alleys and sidewalks with a hose. This made an oil slick in the gutters, which caused the environmentalists on the Logan porch to complain bitterly. All this resulted in eventually converting to a gas furnace. But in the meantime, it was a nightmare. Yet through it all, He remained our Most High God.

He was in control during the difficulties in our family, which took several years to heal, but now things are better than ever thanks to our Most High God.

He was even in control when I returned from the Logan in September of 1990 to hear that Mom had cancer, and I was wondering if I'd be available to take care of her when she really needed me. Would my increasing dizziness incapacitate me? Would I have to be at the Logan in New Jersey when I needed to be with her in Rockville, Maryland? These questions were always on my mind. El Elyon intervened in every case.

Mom became bedridden on March 10, 1991. God enabled me to take care of her at home. Never having taken care of a dying person before, I didn't know if I was able. It was especially hard because it was my own Mom!

The hospice people were wonderful. They taught me how to do things that I didn't think I was capable of doing and they were always just a phone call away. They helped us to arrange for a night nurse to come in for the 11:00 p.m. to 7:00 a.m. shift. She turned out to be a Christian and read Scripture and prayed for Mom as well. Mom rarely slept because her heart was racing so badly. As I left each night, I would reassure her that "joy would come in the morning" (see Ps. 30:5). (She used to call me her "Joy.") The Lord gave me the grace to cheerfully take care of her needs during the day, and then I would cry all the way home each night.

One of the Scriptures God gave me during that time was from Isaiah 41:10: "Do not fear, for I am with you; do not anxiously look about you, for I am your God. I will strengthen you, surely I will help you, surely I will uphold you with My righteous right hand." I shared that verse with Mom back in September when she first found out the seriousness of her condition.

One morning in early March when I came into her room, she said, "Guess what verse I read this morning?" She held up her boney little fist and said triumphantly, "I will uphold you with My righteous right hand." Mom's enduring faith was a beacon to her family, to the folks at the Logan, and to all the Sunday school pupils she had taught from the time she was a teenager.

As time wore on, Mom knew that her time was getting short. As we discussed it one day, I reminded her of Psalm 107, where the Lord promises to bring us into His "desired haven." She found comfort in those words.

Taking care of my 76-year-old mother was all-consuming. At the end of each long day, I would go home, take a shower, and fall into bed. Six a.m. came early. Our daughter Kristi had come to visit her grandma one day during her illness. I usually left little gifts on our kids' beds when they came to visit. This time, of course, her bed was empty. I knew that she would understand. We enjoyed her short visit, even though I knew that it was hard for her to see her grandmother in such poor condition. When the night nurse arrived later that evening, I kissed Mom good night and drove the short distance back to my house. Numb with physical and emotional exhaustion, I wearily climbed up the steps and walked down the hall to our bedroom. Larry was still downstairs watching the evening news. Walking into the room I noticed that someone had left a little gift on my pillow. "How thoughtful," I said. "Kristi must have dropped it off before she left to go back home!" Opening the little present, I was surprised to see a precious devotional written especially for people who sorrow. A little tear trickled down my cheek.

"Oh Lord," I said, "I'm so tired tonight. Is there just a little something I can read before I go to bed?" I opened to the center of the book. My eyes fell on the Scripture for that day. It was Psalm 107:30: "...He guided them to their desired haven." God's presence bathed my broken heart that night as I was reminded once again that even though things seemed to be out of control, He was higher still.

Only God could have given me the physical, emotional, and spiritual strength I needed during that very hard time in our lives. Through it all, He strengthened, helped, and upheld me just as He promised (see Is. 41:10).

Early on Easter Sunday, March 31, 1991, Mom's ultimate joy did come in the morning as she went to be with Jesus. (We later discovered that a year before this, she had told a friend that she thought it would be neat for a Christian to die on Easter. God gave her the desire of her heart.)

Knowing that my Most High God was taking care of my basket full of troubles enabled me to face the challenges that were yet to be revealed.

"Lord, no matter how high our troubles stack, You are higher still. Sometimes it seems like our troubles are piled so high we can't see where we are headed, much less how we are going to get there. No matter what, *we must trust!* Where else can we go but to our Most High God who turns our valleys of 'Trouble' into doors of hope (see Hos. 2:15)–in Jesus' name we pray, amen."

Memories From the Attic

The Lord tells us to work for His glory and purpose, and not to do things for man's approval. This principle was ground into me throughout my time at the Logan. I believe that, as a follower of Christ, I am to be holy just as He is holy (see 1 Pet. 1:16). I think this holiness applies to every detail of my life. In Ecclesiastes, I am told that whatever my hand finds to do, I should do it with all my might (see Eccles. 9:10 NKJ). My mind-set when cleaning the rooms was a desire to do the best job that I could. Also, that "best job" was not to be done with an ungrateful attitude, nor from a motive of seeking approval or praise from others. The imprint left on my heart and mind was to seek the Lord in everything–to make everything I do, think, or say a living and breathing testimony of His love for me and to be a fragrant offering, the aroma of Christ to those who are being saved and those who are perishing (see 2 Cor. 2:14-16 NKJ). That fragrance is to seep through every pore of my being, right down to how I clean a toilet, scrub a floor clean of every sand granule, answer the phone, or think of someone else. The responsibilities of sharing with meal preparations and clean up for us Loganettes in addition to the regular tasks of cleaning and managing the hotel have helped to prepare me for life. God has used these experiences to train me to work hard wherever He places me, and He has given me the principle of a job well done for His glory. Not only did the Lord use those years in Ocean City to mold my spiritual life, but He also prepared me in the practical arenas of my future life.

Patricia Rice '90-'98

Chapter 19

Leaning on My Beloved

Trust in the Lord with all your heart, and do not lean on your own understanding. In all your ways acknowledge Him, and He will make your paths straight (Proverbs 3:5-6).

"Lord, people might think I've had a heart attack in the parking lot," I prayed in muffled tones. I had put my head between my knees and stared at the rubber mat on the floorboard of my car, hoping to recover from another wave of dizziness.

After a few moments, I slowly raised my head and reached down for the lever to draw my seat closer to the steering wheel. Turning the key, I started the motor. Carefully, I drove myself home, realizing that I should no longer be behind the wheel of a car.

Slowly events unfolded that brought me to a place where I had to trust God more than ever—events that led me to the neurologist's office in November of 1991. He had called me in to discuss the results of a recent M.R.I. I never expected to hear such shocking news! He said, "Mrs. Coffin, you have a tumor in the lining of your brain called a miningeoma. You'll have to go to a neurosurgeon and schedule a craniotomy." He continued to speak, while I sat motionless in a fog of disbelief.

How unsettling it was to hear that a foreign object had silently grown to the size of a large grape inside my head! It was too weird for words; it was like something from *The Twilight Zone*!

I put my hand behind my left ear as the doctor explained the position of the tumor. "So that's why I feel dizzy when I try to sing high notes in church," I said, trying to piece it all together.

It all seemed like a dream–a very bad dream! While Larry drove me home that day, I sat in a daze and tried to grasp the reality of the doctor's words.

The days that followed were a blur. And the nights–I dreaded those endless nights when I wrestled with fear in the darkness of despair.

My once-sweet sleep was replaced by nightmares. "The Horrors of Brain Surgery" flashed across the screen of my mind almost nightly. Frequent flashbacks caused me to relive that day several weeks before when the refrigerator had seemed to lift up off the floor and fly over my head, causing me to fall backwards. Praise the Lord that He had His angels there to catch me so I didn't get hurt. It felt to me as if I had fallen on feathers, even though the sound of it startled a visiting neighbor who came running in from the next room to see what had happened. With her assistance, I crawled to the couch in the living room.

My world had literally turned upside down in those moments, and my ability to walk unassisted became a thing of the past. I remember going to the hospital when that first CAT scan failed to detect the intruder that was lurking in the dark recesses of the lining of my brain. Disappointed and still reeling from the fall, I had to lean hard on my beloved Larry in more ways than one, as we walked down the hallway to the emergency room exit.

A verse, Song of Solomon 8:5, came to mind. It couldn't have been more perfect, "Who is this coming up from the wilderness, leaning on her beloved?..." It really was a time that I had to lean on Jesus, my Beloved, more than ever! I could no longer "lean on my own understanding," that's for sure (see Prov. 3:5)!

It wasn't until I was sent for that M.R.I. that the silent intruder was revealed. In the meantime, some of the most severe dizziness had subsided, for which I was grateful. I seemed to have the most difficulty when it was dark and I was in wide open spaces like shopping malls.

The words of the neurosurgeon were reassuring. "Miningeomas are not usually malignant, so it will be okay to wait a little while before surgery," he said. That meant that I could get through Christmas and Chip and Brenda's wedding in January before going to the hospital on February 14, 1991. (I worried about being well enough to take care of my Mom in the last stages of lung cancer.) We picked that date from the ones the doctor offered us because people would remember the date easily to pray for me. Kristi, who has a Valentine birthday, said, "Mom, how could you?" But she understood.

Meanwhile, fear continued to eat me alive. One day, as I sat with my Bible in my lap, I made a declaration, "There's life beyond the tumor!" If I die, I go to Heaven and have eternal life! If I live through it, with God's grace, I'll also have a life on the other side of this. With that bold declaration of faith, fear was disarmed. It's like satan holds those carrots of fear in front of us to run us ragged. That is, he does so until we decide to trust God. As I met fear head on with Jesus, satan's carrot fell off the stick!

I was always aware that fear was behind a closed door. I could open it at any time. But I never did; I was enjoying the peace of God that surpasses all understanding, too much (see Phil. 4:7). And then, the most embarrassing thing happened. I got filled with joy! People looked at me pretty funny when I excitedly told them I was facing a craniotomy! That's okay. I'd take peace and joy any day instead of fear. God is so good!

The day before my surgery, I woke up with an infection in both eyes! Now, I know that they don't operate on you with an infection of any kind. I went into my front bedroom and prayed a desperate prayer. "Lord, we sent out 2,000 Logan letters asking people to pray for this on Valentine's Day. Lord, You know I need to get better so that I can take care of my Mom! I also need to be well enough to open the Logan in the spring." Then, relinquishing everything into His hands, I prayed, "But Lord, I'll continue to trust You whether I go to surgery tomorrow or not! I know You are in control!" As I laid my potentially unfulfilled expectations on His altar, warm, salty tears poured out of my bloodshot eyes. Suddenly as a new level of peace rose up within me, these words from Psalm 28:7 (KJV) came to mind: "My heart trusted in Him, and I am helped." I got up off of my knees and walked down the hall to our bedroom. When I looked at Larry, he said, "Joyce, your eyes have been healed!" It was as if the infection had been washed away by my tears of relinquishment. We hugged one another and rejoiced in the faithfulness of our God.

I came to the hospital the next day on eagle's wings. (There was probably no need for a gurney, but I used one anyway.) God's peace remained steadfast in my heart as that door of fear remained permanently closed.

After the surgery, the neurosurgeon met Larry in the surgical waiting room. He said, "I destroyed the acoustic nerve in the process of removing the tumor. I'm sorry to say that Joyce is deaf in the left ear." Relieved that it was all over, Larry replied, "That's okay. I am deaf in my right ear. We'll just be bookends!"

When Larry came into the intensive care unit, he kissed me on the forehead and announced, "The doctor said that you are deaf in the left ear." Then, I said the worst thing I could have possibly said. "What did you say?" (By my response, he thought for sure that the doctor was right.) But by the grace of God, I could still hear! The surgeon came in and asked me if I could hear him rub his fingers together next to my left ear. I said, "Yes." He stroked his goatee and said, "It's a mystery." I said, "It's a miracle!" (I figured a neurosurgeon knew an acoustic nerve when he saw one.)

I felt such an anointing the whole time I was in the hospital. Everyone who came in the door heard about my miracle and looked amazed. I too continued to be amazed! I thank God that there are no ill-effects from my surgery. The "grape" has never returned! Praise the Lord!

There is no doubt in my mind that Jesus, the same yesterday, today, and tomorrow (see Heb. 13:8), is still in the business of healing. He could have healed my tumor beforehand, but He chose to do a new thing. "Who is this coming up from the wilderness, leaning [not on her own understanding but] on her beloved?" (Song 8:5) It's me!

"Dear wonderful, faithful Lord, may we all have ears to hear Your voice! We look back on the wilderness times in our lives knowing that we couldn't have made it without leaning on our Beloved. In Your own hour of testing, You said, '...Father, if Thou art willing, remove this cup from Me; yet not My will, but Thine be done' (Lk. 22:42). As we submit to Your perfect will, give us the grace to face the future knowing there is always 'life' beyond whatever comes! In Jesus' name we pray, amen."

Memories From the Attic

I remember going to Good News Club at Joyce's house in Rockville and praying the prayer with her to accept Jesus into my heart. That was a great start, but it wasn't really until my senior high years and my days at the Logan that the Lord really began to mean something to me in a powerful and personal way.

My parents, especially my mom, laid a wonderful foundation for me as I grew up in a Christian home. I was always expected to attend church and Bible studies regularly. What a nice feeling it was when that all became something that I truly wanted to do. The Logan helped to make that possible, and in so many ways it was there as a beacon of light in my life. Joyce's able sidekick, Carol Clements, was a bright spot too. I treasure my friendship with Kristi as well. I thank the Lord for all these ladies and for their help in nurturing my relationship with the Lord.

As I reflect on those years at the Logan, there are so many memorable things; it is hard to single out just one. When I think of the Logan, I think of all the love there, and of course, Joyce and Larry. The Saturday night sing-alongs were a constant, and they were followed up by a stroll on the boardwalk. I remember the early Bible studies that we were not always thrilled to get up for, but we were always glad we did once we were awake. We also were grateful for the opportunity to go off for a quiet time before starting our morning work. I remain grateful to Joyce and Larry for showing us that discipline.

Jeanne (Ostrander) Cooper '83-'86

Chapter 20

In Light of Eternity

Let each one do just as he has purposed in his heart; not grudgingly or under compulsion; for God loves a cheerful giver (2 Corinthians 9:7).

"Clinging to material things has never been one of my problems," I boasted to my friend over a hot cup of tea one afternoon. Little did I know that God would use my husband's gift of giving to cause me to eat my words.

The Logan was fully furnished when we bought it. The linen closets were stocked, the beds were made, there were figurines on the shelves (all but the Hummel figurines, which the Meyers took when they left, of course), and wicker chairs still lined the big front porch.

The guests just loved to sit in those barrel-backed chairs to catch the ocean breezes. For as far back as we can remember, they had been painted a pale green. In more recent years, we had painted them white to match the railings, and of course, we've had to recover the overstuffed cushions several times.

"You know, Joyce," commented a guest one day while running her hand along the contour of one of the chairs,

"They don't make wicker like this anymore. These are very valuable chairs!"

I began to have a new appreciation for those wicker chairs from that day forward.

Then came the test! Before that summer was over, Larry had given away several of those "valuable" wicker chairs! (When God moves on my husband's heart to give, he does so without a moment's hesitation.)

"That's Larry for you," I said to one of the recipients through a phoney smile that reminded me of the old days. "Oh well, Lord, I know that everything we have is really Yours," I prayed to myself, wiping a little tear from my cheek as if God might not have noticed.

In the fall, I looked forward to coming back to our Maryland home to become a full-time wife again. Just as in the years past, things seemed so different after being gone for almost four months. My eyes adjusted to take in the familiar surroundings that had taken on a strange newness.

As in all the years before, I wandered through my home like I was on some kind of house tour. Walking down the steps to our family room, I noticed that something was definitely missing. "Honey, where's the couch?" I asked my husband, almost afraid to hear the answer.

"Oh yeah, I gave it to our niece. She needed something to sit on in the horse barn when she puts on her riding boots," Larry called from the kitchen in his practical, matter-of-fact way.

"You did what?" I responded with a mixture of unbelief and anger rising up inside of me. Thoughts of my couch caked with horsehair, mud, and manure started to turn my stomach.

"How could you do it?" I asked him. He stood there speechless. My adrenaline was really pumping as I threw myself into the task of unpacking!

Once again, a divinely inspired flashback caught my attention. Regretfully, I recalled that conversation with my friend when I had pridefully declared, "Clinging to material things has never been one of my problems." I quietly gulped at the memory.

I fell to my knees by my bed. "Dear Father, You didn't even withhold Your only Son! Yet here I am, clinging to silly wicker chairs and mud-caked couches! Thank You for using my husband's strong points to reveal my weak ones. I confess the sin of the idolatry in my life. After all, everything I have belongs to You. Please make me into a cheerful giver."

Afterward, I went down to Larry, asked him to forgive my bad attitude, and thanked him for being such a wonderful, generous husband. And we didn't even have a problem finding something else to sit on in the rec room that evening. (And the empty spot made a perfect place for my ironing board.)

In light of eternity, couches and wicker chairs have a way of losing their importance.

* * *

One of the most giving people I have ever met is Robby Janssen. The selflessness of Christ shines from his life in such a way that you feel bathed in God's love just to know him.

You may have seen him at the Logan. He's the tall, lanky guy with long blond hair who breezes in and out of the hotel like the wind. If you haven't seen him, he was probably on some distant shore sharing the love of Jesus through missions. Hundreds of teenagers have benefitted from his godly example through Young Life, Son Servants, and the

Fellowship of Christian Athletes (not to mention all the people who have been involved with the hotel).

We first met Robby shortly after buying the Logan. One of our girls "ran into him" on the track (no pun intended). Ellen (Scroggs) Walton had gone to Western Maryland College with Robby. She was so glad to see him again that she brought him across the street to meet us at the Logan. Little did we know it at the time, but Robby and his family would become like family to us!

After his parents sold their house on East Atlantic Avenue in 1988, and his five siblings went in different directions, Robby stayed on ministering to the Ocean City kids he loved so much. After a summer season of being a live-in helper to an elderly woman, he moved in with us, serving as the winter caretaker of the Logan and as a right hand for Larry, helping with the endless upkeep and repairs. As you can probably tell by now, Robby holds a very special place in the Coffin quiver. God is so good.

Robby's healthy eating habits radiate the fruit of self-control and are a source of constant conviction for those who don't have it. There is not one organic morsel that he wouldn't gladly give away to anyone who looks slightly interested.

I don't mean to put Robby on a pedestal, but it does our hearts good to see such a humble young man of God who is so totally sold out to Him. The few earthly possessions Robby owns are kept in Room 3 at the Logan, where he lives year round (when he's not on the mission field). If his clothes seem a little tattered, it's probably because he has given the nicer ones away to those who needed them more than he does. His humble devotion to Jesus is the most important thing in his life. May God bless this "cheerful giver" a hundredfold for the blessing he has been to others. May we all learn from him.

"Dear Lord, thank You for sending godly examples into our lives to remind us that the most important treasures are really stored in Heaven. Help us to prioritize our lives so that we too hold nothing dear except for those things that count for eternity—in Jesus' name we pray, amen."

Set your mind on the things above, not on the things that are on earth. For you have died and your life is hidden with Christ in God (Colossians 3:2-3).

Memories From the Attic

Late-night talks in the attic were always an adventure. Since I grew up not having a sister, I would get my fill during the summers at the Logan. We would have some deep discussions in the attic, with topics ranging from the cute boys we saw on the beach to the spiritual things that God was teaching us in our daily walk. When you have eight girls living together in a dorm-like place, life is never dull. I'll never forget my friend falling backwards into a laundry basket as she was getting dressed one morning or my cousin accidentally putting her backside through one of the attic windows. For many summers, I would frighten the other girls by talking and walking in my sleep. This was a potentially dangerous situation because the stairs going up to the attic are almost straight up. God protected me all those years from falling "down the hatch."

Everything we did upstairs was supposed to be done quietly, especially after 10:00 p.m. This made things even funnier when we were supposed to be talking with "Logan voices" (as my mother put it). This meant that if we disturbed any of the guests, we would be in hot water with the bosses. Since these bosses were my parents, I didn't get away with much. However, we did manage to "short sheet" friends who were guests from time to time. We always wished that we could be a fly on the wall and actually see their faces when they climbed into bed and realized that they couldn't put their feet straight out.

Kristi (Coffin) Ivosevich '73-'85

One of the neat things about being at the Logan was meeting people. I didn't always know the other chambermaids, but after sharing one meal together, we were friends. That was due to

Joyce's ever-popular "Let's go around the table and share something that..." tradition. She was always very creative in her desire to introduce the newcomers so that we all felt like family.

I remember taking a challenge that Joyce had given all the girls one morning at Bible study. She had been teaching us about witnessing to others. She said that we didn't always have to use the spoken word. In fact, she suggested writing a message in the sand early in the morning. So one morning I arose early and went to the beach. The sand was still untouched by footprints that early. I picked a Scripture verse from the Psalms about the joy of the Lord and began writing it with my feet. Each letter was about six feet high–big enough to read from the boardwalk. I'll never know if those words touched another's soul that morning, but God used it to bless me.

Ellen (Jones) Zell '80-'84

Chapter 21

Pockets of Blessing

That their hearts may be encouraged, having been knit together in love, and attaining to all the wealth that comes from the full assurance of understanding, resulting in a true knowledge of God's mystery, that is, Christ Himself, in whom are hidden all the treasures of wisdom and knowledge (Colossians 2:2-3).

As I was searching for a good title for this chapter, the Lord brought to mind these memories from the pockets of my past.

Kids usually have great imaginations. I was no exception. My favorite pastime was a rare form of "mountain climbing" and "cave exploration."

I grew up in an apartment in Washington, D.C. We didn't own a car or go on many vacations in those days, so I had to be creative. My "mountain" was made by dropping a comforter in such a way that many little "caves" were formed. These made great places to tuck in little treasures like dolls, ceramic puppies, and other knickknacks. Sometimes this assorted array of tiny toys could be seen peeking out of their pockets. Other times I would hide them deep inside. Then I would try to guess where they were, exploring each "cave" with my little hand. (I guess it was like an earlier version of the game "Concentration.") After playing for a while, I would leave my creation behind and run off to do something else. The longer I was away, the better. After all, childish distraction could cause a little girl to forget. The intrigue was heightened when I returned to my comforter that was brimming with so many surprises.... It's amazing how those little pockets of treasure brought such pleasure!

Pockets of blessing are not just reserved for the young. I believe that the good Lord loves to tuck treasures into the pockets of our lives. No matter how old we are, it's still fun to discover them! Let me tell you about one of the manifold treasures that God has tucked into our lives at the Logan Hotel.

It all started with a phone call that came into the front desk in the spring of 1983.

"Hello, this is Elsie Hoffman. Would you be willing to take in a group of mentally challenged adults for a few days?" After hesitating for a moment, I told her that I would call her back after I discussed the matter with Larry. I took down her name and number and hung up the phone. Unanswered questions fluttered around in my mind like a batch of butterflies.

How would the other guests feel about it? Would these special guests be well-behaved? Would they be well-supervised? After Larry and I prayed about it, we knew that God wanted them to come.

I'm sure that you realize by now that I "checked into the Logan" in the early '70's with some very old baggage. The "baggage" I am referring to this time is the problem I had (and still have from time to time) of "what will people think?" However, Ephesians 4:23-24 tells us to "put off the old and put on the new" (my paraphrase). Well, I had lugged around that particular old baggage for so long that I couldn't wait to put it off for something new!

Locating her number, I reluctantly called Mrs. Hoffman back. (I still had reservations about these reservations!)

She reassured me that her people would be well-supervised. When the reservations were made for the end of the season, I was relieved. I knew that there would be fewer guests at the Logan at that time. Then, she went on to tell me how she and her husband Joe had been led by the Lord to take on this ministry.

They had previously worked in a place where these young people had been residents. Unable to teach them about Jesus on the job, they decided to "take them home" as their own foster kids. They purchased an old funeral home in Pennsylvania, and before long, the whole "family" was under one roof. They lovingly called their new home "R House." Finally, Elsie and Joe were free to teach the ways of the Lord to the people they had grown to love so much. The story touched my heart so much that by the time she was finished, I was really looking forward to their visit! I couldn't wait to relate the details of the story the next time Larry called from Rockville.

Mid-September is one of our favorite times of the year. The weather is great. The evenings are cool, the reservations are few, everything is marked down on the boardwalk, and best of all, Larry is able to stay at the Logan full time. The chambermaids are back to school by then so their "shuttle service" to Maryland is temporarily suspended until the following June!

The day came for our special guests to arrive. We watched as nine young people paraded into the lobby. Three adults, including Mrs. Hoffman, helped with their luggage. I was really impressed by the young people's good manners.

When Elsie came up to the desk to check them in, she looked as sweet as I had imagined her to be. The first thing she said was, "Joyce, I have some bad news. My husband Joe passed away in June. It's been very hard, but I know that he is with Jesus now and we'll all be together one day." Before I could ask her any questions, she volunteered, "With the support of my wonderful staff, I'm determined to carry on the work that God has given me."

"How I admire your faithfulness," I said. This woman reminded me of Corrie ten Boom.

The next morning, she came down for coffee. As we chatted in the lobby, one of the guys came down the stairs and asked if he had to make his bed. "Oh, no," I said, "this is your vacation. We'll make it for you." He immediately turned around and started back up the stairs. One of the aides asked where he was going. "I'm going upstairs to unmake my bed!" he said emphatically.

The rooms were spotless as we went in to tidy up each day. Even though they were on vacation, they decided to make their beds after all. (I guess they didn't want to get out of practice.)

One of the gals was so serious all the time. She always looked angry. One day when the group came back from dinner, I greeted them and said, "Hey Debra, what did you have for dinner?"

"Snake!" she growled. (From then on, I didn't ask.)

One afternoon there was a big commotion out back in the showers. I heard squealing and hysterical laughing. I knew the staff was with them. They too were howling. Curiosity getting the best of me, I ran down the hall to the landing that overlooked the showers.

"What's happening?" I shouted, trying to make my voice heard above the racket.

Emma Jones, one of the adult leaders, controlled her laughing long enough to yell up to me, "Debra hates to get her hair washed! She pushed past us, and because she was so soapy, she kept slipping out of our hands." Emma rolled her eyes, shook her head, and continued, "She ran from one shower stall to another trying to escape, but we finally caught her! The funniest part of all is that the guys were lined up along the fence here wide-eyed taking in the whole thing. And Albert, the shy one, yells out 'Whoo...what a body!' She stopped and tried to compose herself. And then she put her hand up to her mouth and said with a softer voice, "Sorry if we are being too loud. But it was just so funny!"

By that time, I was laughing hysterically too. "Snake woman" of all people! It still makes me laugh to think of it. (It also makes me grateful that no other guests were around that day.)

Every evening devotions were held on the front porch. This included singing and prayer. A "joyful noise" could be heard for blocks around. No one hit the same note at the same time, but they sang their hearts out. I know that it was a sweet aroma to the Lord!

The most touching part of their visit came the last night they were there. As I was working behind the desk in the lobby, one of the young men came in and invited Larry and me to join them. Thanking him for the invitation, I went to find Larry. Trying to hurry, I became aware of some "old baggage" that hindered my speed. Thoughts about what the neighbors might think began raising their ugly heads.

A gentle prodding counteracted my fleshly response. These words were impressed on my heart: "*You're going to miss a blessing!*" By the time I found Larry I said, "We've been invited to join them on the porch for devotions. I think God really wants us to go. If we don't, we are going to miss a blessing!"

Hand in hand, we went out onto the porch where the group was already sitting in a circle. Two empty chairs were waiting for us. We joined in the singing of some "not so familiar" hymns. Then it was time to pray.

Now, Larry was still wearing his neck brace as a result of recent disc surgery (one of the five he's experienced in his lifetime). Nothing had been said about it. We didn't think that they noticed. The people took turns praying. After a few minutes, the young guy sitting next to Larry put his hand on his shoulder and began to pray boldly with a shaky voice, "Lord, heal this man!" When it was our turn, we could hardly speak. We were too overcome by the blessing we had come very close to missing.

* * *

Tucked back inside this pocket of blessing was something I just recently discovered. I found out that 16 years later, "R House" is still going strong. Elsie and Joe are both in Heaven now cheering on their daughter Charlotte who has taken over the ministry. Emma still lovingly refers to "R House" as her family. We do too!

"Dear Lord, please rid us of the baggage of the past that blocks Your blessings. It's amazing to think that the Creator of the universe takes time to tuck treasures into the fabric of our lives. Thank You for sending us Your Comforter. We can't wait for the Holy Spirit to reveal those hidden treasures You have that are just waiting to be discovered. Thank You so much for each pocket of blessing You have planned for us along the way–in Jesus' name we pray, amen."

Memories From the Attic

I remember:

- *The time that Robby's dad went home to be with Jesus.*
- *The time Joyce told us to reach out to a girl whose back hurt. After feeding her lunch and putting a heating pad on her back, we found out that the hurt person was really her sister.*
- *The time my sister Noel asked the people she was checking in if they were "coffee dinkles."*
- *The time a guest "doctored" our geraniums, and they ended up looking like little sticks coming from the pots.*
- *The time Gary and Sharon fell in love, and the times we had sing-along instrumentals.*
- *The golf tournaments, ladies' and singles' retreats, and the many hurricanes.*
- *The summers I planted herbs out on the back deck.*
- *"Experiencing God" summers, and learning about temperaments.*
- *The summer the temperature hit 100 degrees and one of the chambermaids forgot to put some of the cans of smelly garbage out front for the pick-up. (She had reassured us it was taken care of.) As a result, Larry decided to carry it home in the Toyota truck. Over an hour down the road, the truck broke down and Joyce got a call to come rescue him. She gladly left in the little Escort to rescue Larry only to realize that she had to rescue hot smelly garbage as well. There was a small space between the trunk and the car and the overwhelming aroma in the sweltering heat made Joyce sick at her stomach. Is this what is meant by "for better or for worse"?*

Emily McDermitt '87-'98

Some of the things I remember about the Logan are the following: scrubbing the outside showers with toothbrushes while singing in harmony with Kristen; Noel in shower cap and rubber gloves changing the linens in a room suspected to be "contagious"; watching a gorgeous sunset from the west attic window with Emily; running on the boardwalk and in the Gardens looking at all the neat homes; biking to the tip of the island for a picnic on the north bay beach with Emily; cleaning Rooms 6 and 7 to the rhythm of tennis balls hitting rackets from across the street; taking pictures of sunsets from the bay as I was developing a love in me for God's masterpiece of creating the sky each day; cleaning Room 16 with background music of Tchaikovsky's "1812 Overture" and Gershwin's "Rhapsody in Blue" coming from the building next door; dreaming of what the hotel was like when first built in 1908, thinking, "If only these walls could speak of what they have beheld and heard"; joining in the sing-a-longs on the front porch; having my prayer and devotion times in "The King's Corner" (a nickname I gave to the small alcove in the front of the hotel attic, which faced northeast and allowed me a view of the sunrises); sleeping in a hammock one night in the attic (not realizing I had broken fire code regulations by blocking the aisle); going around the table games during dinner time, and seeing the red geraniums on the front porch.

Patricia Rice '90-'98

Chapter 22

Picture Perfect

As for God, His way is perfect....It is God who arms me with strength and makes my way perfect (Psalm 18:30,32 NIV).

The Logan has some very unique pictures that you'd appreciate even more if you knew the stories behind them.

Take, for instance, the red heart made from intricately cut Chinese characters. It was given to us by Donna Lam, our "adopted daughter" from the Orient. People who aren't familiar with Mandarin may not be aware that these characters are actually a few verses taken from the love chapter, First Corinthians 13, which remains a constant reminder of how the blood of Jesus binds together people from "...every tribe and tongue and people and nation" (Rev. 5:9).

The bronze profile of Christ that hangs in the stairwell of the Logan is really the entire Book of John etched in letters so minute that you need a strong magnifying glass to read it.

Another one of our treasures hangs in the Logan lobby. It's a watercolor painting of the Ocean City Music Pier created by one of our talented Logan Ladies, Emily McDermitt, when she was only a senior in high school.

The painting of the ocean waves breaking on the shore with a driftwood-like frame was painted by Larry's sister, Kay Singleton, who took her first painting lessons when she was 60 years old. (Her husband Tommy made the frame.) Over the years they have left other tender-loving touches at the Logan as well.

The picture of shepherds watching over their sheep under a navy blue star-studded sky has a really neat story behind it. I had just seen it in a Bible bookstore in Maryland, where I had stood admiring it for a long time. The picture, a painting by R.J. Watson, was called "Starry Night" and was taken from Ruth Bell Graham's book, *One Wintery Night*. I loved the way the stars seemed to twinkle in the special lighting effects. After looking at the price tag, I quickly went on my way knowing I couldn't "afford" to look any longer. The next evening, we had a farewell dinner for Diane, a lawyer friend from the Ocean City area, who had been staying with us in Rockville while she worked on a special assignment. After dinner, she ran up to her room to get a thank-you gift that she had bought for us several weeks before. Imagine the shock I had as I unwrapped the present and saw shepherds and twinkling stars winking at me through the tissue paper! The painting was exactly like the one I had secretly admired the night before! I love it when God gives us the "desires of our hearts" in the first place so that He can meet them in the second place (see Ps. 37:4b)!

There is also the picture of a bird perched over a thundering waterfall on the limb of a white birch tree. The print was etched into a piece of pine by a wood-burning tool and beautifully painted with muted watercolors. It was given to us by some very special guests, the Martins, in the summer of 1977. I immediately took a liking to the picture. Besides the fact that I like waterfalls, there was something very peaceful about the picture. I loved how the white birch trees were silhouetted against the stormy sky.

About a week after receiving it, I was in the bathtub reading a little devotional booklet called *Our Daily Bread*. (God speaks to me in the most unusual places sometimes.) Turning to July 26, 1977, my eyes fell on a story entitled, "Peace in the Storm" by Henry Bosch.[1] It was about a contest where artists were asked to portray a picture of "peace." The prizewinner depicted a small bird perched on a limb over a thundering waterfall. In spite of the noise and the impending storm, the bird remained unruffled. I cut the story out and taped it to the back of my picture where it remains to this day. (Perhaps God was telling us, years ago, that even in the midst of the coming storms, He would be *Jehovah Shalom*, our peace.) By the way, the devotional Scripture for that day read, "Thou wilt keep him in perfect peace, whose mind is stayed on thee" (Is. 26:3a KJV).

Time and time again, people have been ministered to by the pictures that just happen to be in their rooms at the Logan. The funny part about it is, I often rearrange them. After staying at a darling bed and breakfast a couple of years ago, I got inspired to change things around at the Logan. We couldn't afford to do much at the time, so I brought a variety of pictures up from our home in Maryland. With my arms full, I ran from room to room, looking to see where each one would fit. (After all, the colors had to complement the rest of the decor!) All along, I thought I was doing my thing! I found out later that I was being directed by the Holy Spirit!

Let me explain. A young woman came to the Logan. She had mailed in her reservations so we had never met face to face. Because she wanted a room with toilet and sink, I put her in Room 14 (the only one I had available). The day came

1. Henry Bosch, "Peace in the Storm," *Our Daily Bread* (July, 1977).

for her to arrive. I never expected anything out of the ordinary as I checked in this attractive young woman. Since it was her first trip to Ocean City, I invited her to go to the boardwalk with me after my shift was over. She agreed to go.

It's funny how you get pictures in your mind of exactly where you were when significant things happen. I remember the two of us walking toward Fifth Street on the boardwalk, enjoying the cool breezes. The setting sun projected beautiful "feather duster" prints of pink and turquoise over the ocean that evening. We admired God's handiwork as we walked along making small talk. Before long, my new friend began to share something that was on her heart. Surprised, I hung on every word.

"Before I came to Ocean City, I prayed for guidance about my job situation," she confided. "I've worked for my company for several years and have been wondering if the time has come for me to move on. You see, I've already received another offer. I know that God is not the author of confusion (see 1 Cor. 14:33 KJV), so the purpose of this trip was to fast and pray about my decision. But, Joyce, I got my answer as soon as I checked into the room and saw the Precious Moments' needlepoint on the wall! It confirmed the fact that God wants me to stay in my present job! You see...I work for Precious Moments!"

Another "picture-perfect" story took place in Room 14 as well. Last year, I replaced the memorable Precious Moments' needlepoint with a dramatic picture of eagles that seemed to "better complement the decor." Isaiah 40:31 (KJV) was inscribed on the bottom: "But they that wait upon the Lord shall renew their strength; they shall mount up with wings as eagles...."

Unlike the early days of June when I have time to redecorate, by mid-season the only walls that get my attention are the wall-to-wall reservations that come pouring in. So by this time, where I put which picture no longer seemed to matter, but it mattered to God!

One of our regular guests returned for a week's vacation in her favorite room (Room 14). She came to the desk to check out when her week was over and looked at me with tears in her eyes and said, "You probably aren't aware of it, Joyce, but I've been taking care of my Dad since his stroke last year. It's really been hard for me to watch him deteriorate right before my eyes." As she struggled to continue, I started getting teary, as I identified closely with her pain.

"It must have been hard to get away for this much-needed vacation," I said while she regained her composure.

"It was very hard, but you know, God has given me a Scripture that has strengthened me through it all. It's Isaiah 40:31." Before I could make the connection she said, "When I saw that same verse on the eagle picture in my room, I knew that God would continue to strengthen me, no matter what the future holds." Once again, God's "handwriting was on the wall"!

"Dear Lord, it's incredible how You orchestrate our seemingly simple actions and perfect them for Your eternal purposes. May we never underestimate Your desire to be intimately involved in our lives–in Jesus' name we pray, amen."

I will instruct you and teach you in the way which you should go; I will counsel you with My eye upon you (Psalm 32:8).

Memories From the Attic

After intense and thought-provoking Bible studies, I usually found myself excited and ready for time alone with the Lord. In those quiet times I remember having strong feelings of peace and understanding of what I was reading in God's Word. My prayer life was enhanced as I began to write my prayers to God in a journal. Not all my quiet times were beneficial at first, and I don't necessarily see that as a bad thing since it was in some of those times that I learned the most. At times I would feel very bitter and uninterested in spending time alone with God. Nevertheless, I would pray to Him and express my negative feelings. Just doing that made me more open to listening to His voice and hearing what He had to say to me, and so it was in my quiet times that My relationship with God was strengthened.

Jenny Parent '91-'99

I have so many great memories of the summers that I've worked at the Logan. I was always challenged spiritually when I was there. The Logan is a unique hotel where both the guests and workers are blessed. One story of answered prayer that I'll always remember is when the hot water heater broke. It was very chilly outside and we didn't want people to have to take cold showers. We prayed about it and before we knew it, it was working!

Elizabeth Wilson '92-'97

Working at the Logan the past three years has been a wonderful blessing. The Logan is a haven of peace, a lighthouse amidst darkness. It is a place where I can spend quality time with God and be encouraged by girls of many ages. The Logan is not only a ministry to the guests, but also to the workers. Joyce and Larry are wonderful parents away from home. It's amazing to see how God works through the smallest of circumstances. When I come home, I feel rejuvenated and have a new thirst for Christ.

Sarah Busick '96-'99

Chapter 23

Zachary

The Lord is my strength and my shield; my heart trusts in Him, and I am helped; therefore my heart exults, and with my song I shall thank Him (Psalm 28:7).

"Good morning, the Logan Hotel!" I glanced at my watch, hoping that it was still morning.

The woman on the other end of the line spoke softly. "Hello. This is Diane Fillman."

"Hi, Diane. How are you?"

"Not so well, Joyce." Her voice trembled. "Our family is going through a very hard time right now."

"Tell me, Diane, what is wrong?"

"Our son Dennis and his wife Michele have been trying to have a baby for several years. They've been disappointed so many times. After resigning themselves to the fact that they couldn't have children of their own, they decided to adopt a baby.

"Four months ago, they adopted a precious baby boy. They named him Seth. He instantly captivated all our hearts. The church family has prayed for this child for so long; they love him as their own." I listened intently as she continued.

"A couple of weeks ago, the case worker called. The kids received a crushing blow when she informed them that the birth father's name had been forged on the legal documents. He is aware that he has a son now, and he wants his baby! Legally, Seth will have to be given over to his biological father." Her voice broke.

"Oh, Diane," I said with tears streaming down my face, "what a heartbreaking story! Is there anything we can do to help?"

"Well, that's why I am calling. Dennis and Michele will be going to Philadelphia next week to hand Seth over to this total stranger!" She swallowed hard before she could continue. "I know they will need to go somewhere to regroup before going back to the empty house. They just love Ocean City, New Jersey, and I immediately thought of the Logan. Would you have a room for four days starting on Tuesday?"

"Of course," I said, trying to regain my composure. I cleared my throat. It was time to think about the business of being an innkeeper again. Looking on the reservation chart, I said, "There is a room available with toilet and shower. I'd be glad to reserve it for them."

"Thank you so much. I'll put a deposit in the mail this afternoon."

"We certainly will be praying for your family, Diane. During times like these we really have to white-knuckle God's faithfulness!"

"We sure do," she replied. "Joyce, I can't tell you how grateful I am that the kids have a haven to come to during the storm. Thanks again. Good-bye."

"Good-bye, dear." The receiver felt heavier than usual as I put it back into the cradle. It felt like the heaviness in my heart. I wrote the name "Fillman" on the chart. If only I could have written "crib" in the space as well....

The night before they were to arrive, I tossed and turned. I prayed for them into the wee hours of the morning. "Lord, You said that You would never give us more than we can handle. (see 1 Cor. 10:13). As Dennis and Michele's Good Shepherd, restore their souls (see Ps. 23:1,3). Carry them on eagles' wings through this valley of trouble (see Ex. 19:4; Hos. 2:15)."

The next day, I was the manager on duty at the front desk. I will never forget seeing the Fillmans coming through the door that day. The agonizing grief that gripped their hearts stared at me through vacant eyes. Not wanting to make it any harder for them, I tried to be as businesslike as possible. "You must be the Fillmans," I said. They nodded.

There were things they needed to know about staying at the Logan. I knew that the last thing they wanted to hear was a long orientation. I frantically looked over the list of check-in information. This day, so many of those things seemed unimportant. I proceeded to acquaint them with the hotel. Halfway through, I almost lost it. I kept picturing them handing over their baby to a complete stranger! *They'll probably never see him again*, I said to myself silently. I kept pushing those heart-wrenching thoughts away. Only by God's grace did the Fillmans and I make it through the preliminaries.

I showed them to their room. After I came down to the kitchen, I fell apart. One of the little chambermaids asked, "Are you all right?"

"No," I sobbed, still feeling so much of the couples' pain. She put her arms around me and hugged me until I regained my composure. (There is such healing in hugs.) I thank God that the phone didn't ring and for sending chambermaids with the gift of mercy.

One question kept plaguing my mind. "Did I do the right thing by not mentioning Seth? They might think I don't care."

I decided to write a note:

> "Dear Dennis and Michele: We just want you to know that we love you. Our prayers are with you during this difficult time. If you need a hug or someone to talk to, we are here for you. Love in Christ, the Logan Staff."

I quietly slipped it under their door, hoping not to disturb them.

Every morning, we saw this sweet little couple sitting in the wicker chairs on the Logan's front porch. They seemed to be soaking up God's strength as they read their Bibles. The note wasn't mentioned. However, they did smile at me every time they passed by.

On the day they were to check out, Dennis and Michele came up to the desk. I introduced them to Larry who had been in Maryland when they checked in. I had already filled him in on what had taken place in Philadelphia.

They started by thanking me for my note, saying how much it had meant to them. Then, as if we were old friends, they shared from the depths of their hearts. We could see that God had truly become their anchor in the storm. The strength they had drawn from Him was very evident.

"We aren't mad at God," said Michele. "We are just so thankful that we could have Seth for four wonderful months. We may have only held him in our arms for a short time, but we'll carry him in our hearts forever." She looked up into the face of her husband standing next to her.

"We don't understand how it will happen, but we know God will bring good out of it somehow," added Dennis with a strong sense of conviction.

Larry and I hugged them as we said good-bye. We cried as we watched them leave, knowing in our hearts that God would help them to face the empty crib and little toys. He would also carry them through the difficult days ahead. We were amazed that those we had hoped to encourage had encouraged us even more....

The next Christmas, we were pleasantly surprised to hear from Dennis and Michele. The following excerpt is from their newsletter:

> "We received a call from our case worker on November 9—would we be interested in showing our profile to a birth couple? After a day's consideration, we called our case worker, YES! Show our profile. On November 16 (it seemed much longer than just a week's wait), we learned that we were to be the parents of a beautiful son who was born October 30, weighing 7 lbs, 10 oz. He was declared 'beautiful' by the pediatrician who saw him 10 days after his birth. The next few weeks were filled with evidences of God at work in making us into a family."

The letter went on to tell that after much prayerful consideration, they had picked a name for their new baby. "We will call him Zachary, because it means, 'Jehovah has remembered.' "As Dennis and Michele went to the agency to pick up their new son, the caseworker told them that the birth parents had already named him. She said, "His name is Zachary!"

"Dear Lord, You have such a wonderful way of turning our valleys of trouble into doors of hope (see Hos. 2:15). You do remember, let us never forget! In Jesus' name we pray, amen."

Memories From the Attic

One time while I was working at the Logan, there were some mentally challenged adults from a group home vacationing there. One fellow always stood out in the group. He was friendly and easygoing and always told everyone that he loved them. The day they checked out, Jeanne and I were doing changeovers together. We got to the room in which this gentleman had stayed, and we began to clean the room. As I went to dust the top of the dresser, I made a startling discovery. Our buddy had left, of all things, his teeth! The worst part was fighting over who was going to remove them from the room, me or Jeanne. I believe it came down to the old "finders keepers" theory, and I took them downstairs and gladly handed them over to Joyce!

Since I sunburned better than anyone, I could always count on Joyce for help. I wonder if Joyce still has that obsession about peeling sunburned skin.

I used to love Fourth of July at the Logan. We always hoped that Joyce had booked someone we knew in one of the rooms that was above the porch, so that we could use their room to climb out on the porch roof to watch the fireworks. I also love the memories of the Saturday night sing-alongs on the front porch of the Logan.

I remember when one of the appliances broke down; I think it was a dryer. Joyce couldn't get someone to repair it right away, and we had laundry that needed to be done. She called all the girls downstairs, and we laid hands on it, and of course, it worked fine after that!

I also remember the time when Jodi and I had our turn to cook, and we decided to make hamburgers. They shrunk up to about the size of a half dollar.

One retreat stands out in my mind. We were split into groups and given a bag full of items. In the bag was also a parable. We had to take the items and use all of them while acting out the parable. I don't recall what our parable was, but I recall that I had to doctor up Ellen Jones by using an Ace bandage and Ben Gay. I still have a picture of Mr. Dick wearing some crazy thing on his head while acting out his skit! What fun that was!

I had so many good times at the Logan, it's hard to pick a few to share. I enjoyed sending seaweed home in letters to friends one summer and picking through a vacuum's bag looking for a contact lens. Most of all, I enjoyed the fellowship with such wonderful people. I thank Joyce and Larry for having such a special place. I must have a special place in my heart for the Logan; I wouldn't have named my firstborn child "Marriott" or "Radisson," but I did name him "Logan"!

Lisa (Baumann) Fletcher '78-'83

Chapter 24

A Thief in Our Midst

...for there is nothing covered that will not be revealed, and hidden that will not be known (Matthew 10:26).

"It looks like an inside job, Ma'am," the policeman told me as I stared at him in disbelief.

My chambermaids have always been beyond reproach. I couldn't believe that one of my girls could have been responsible for this rash of robberies at the Logan! I thought of each precious girl individually.

I trust each one of them implicitly! They're like my own kids! The officer has got to be wrong! But if it wasn't an "inside job," who could have been responsible? I pondered.

We had owned the Logan for 20 years by this time. Nothing like this had ever happened before. Now, my own chambermaids were missing money and articles of clothing from the attic. Guests were complaining about missing cash. Each time something was reported, I convinced myself that the individuals must have been mistaken. *Perhaps the things have just been misplaced,* I tried to console myself. Finally, the evidence became overwhelming. "There's a thief in our midst!" I finally admitted, as I dialed the local police department.

The policeman came quickly. He interviewed all my girls and then scratched his head. "I can't understand it. All the evidence points to an inside job, but the girls who work here seem to be so honest. We'll just have to wait and see," he said. I thanked him and watched as he walked down the front steps to his squad car. We still had no answers.

The next day, I was still reeling with shock over the events of the past couple of days. I was afraid to go behind the desk for fear that I would hear more bad news. That afternoon, I made the decision to fast and pray about the situation. After checking the chart for an available room, I went down the hall to Room 4. It's funny how you have mental snapshots about things like this. I closed the door and sat on the floor. (Sitting on the made beds is a no-no for fear of messing up the "works of art.")

As I thought about teachings on the blood covenant, I recalled the benefits of being in covenant with the Lord. First of all, it is one-sided. God does all the work, and we are the grateful recipients. Our possessions are His. Our enemies are His. Our problems are His problems. It actually resembles a marriage covenant, but the covenant we have with God is sealed in the blood of Jesus. It actually should be taken even more seriously!

There, on the floor of Room 4, I spoke to the Lord like I never had before. With a great deal of frustration, I said, "I thought we were supposed to be in covenant with one another, Lord! I've prayed and prayed for wisdom, yet You remain silent. You know how upset I am about these robberies! Maybe You are speaking, and I'm too upset to hear Your voice. I will fast until I do." By this time, I was sobbing. Emotionally spent, I went back down the hall to Room 5 and threw myself across my bed.

A couple of hours later, I was awakened from a sound sleep with the words, "Arise and eat" (see 1 Kings 19:5). "But I'm fasting!" I said. Supposing it to be the tempter, I rolled over and went back to sleep. A few moments later, it came again. "Arise and eat." There was a sudden awareness that it was the Lord speaking. There had been a breakthrough in the spiritual realm. But the victory that was ours was yet to be unfolded. I got up and celebrated by eating a bagel!

Within a day or two, the puzzle pieces started to fall into place. One of the things that was missing was a $40 gift certificate that I had bought for my friend, Sharon Griffith, who had come over to the Logan to work for me one evening. I knew that she wouldn't accept money, so I decided to give her a gift certificate from B & B (a clothing store on Asbury Avenue). I was so mad at myself for misplacing it amidst the turmoil. Figuring I could always use it if the first one eventually showed up, I went back to get another one. It's amazing that the same girl who had helped me before was working that afternoon. "Didn't you just get a $40 gift certificate for Sharon Griffith?" she asked. "Yes, I did, but I misplaced it so I thought that I'd get another one," I explained. "But someone came in a couple of days ago to cash it in!" she said. I asked her to describe the girl. (I thought perhaps I had somehow sent it to Sharon after all.) But the description did not match Sharon Griffith. I ran back to the Logan to get a picture of my Logan girls. After showing it to the salesgirl, she made a positive identification.

Our Covenant Partner had come through once again! He was with us during the unfolding of the rest of the drama–meeting with the detectives, confronting the thief, trying to make restitution the best we could out of our own pockets, and dealing with the forgiveness and grief of being betrayed by one of my precious girls.

I still pray for that young lady. She no longer has a place on the Logan staff, of course, but she still has a place in my heart. I'm left with a sense of awe as I think of the place we have in the heart of God as His children in covenant. Something tells me that we have only just begun to skim the surface of all that it means to be His covenant kids!

"Dear heavenly Father, we are so grateful for the times You come through for us. Being in covenant with You is the best security system we could ever have. We hunger for a deeper knowledge of what Your blood covenant means in our lives. May we find insight with understanding as we 'arise and eat' Your Word. In Jesus' name we pray, amen."

Memories From the Attic

Another great benefit of the Logan was learning basic housekeeping. This included, among other things, cooking. When I first came to the Logan, as was the case for most Loganettes, I knew little about cooking meals, especially for 10-20 people! There were many memories there.

I remember Jeannie Roorda's "Golden Bake," a huge 18-inch diameter metal bowl filled with mashed potatoes and carrots and dotted with sausage, then baked until golden. Usually, this meal served 75 so we had enough to freeze. (If something was frozen so long that frostbite made it unrecognizable, we labeled the item "UFOs"–Unidentified Frozen Objects.)

Other kitchen memories include Pressly Ann's sourdough; Karin Rice's poppy seed bread; and Sarah Busick's never-ending supply of chocolate chip cookies.

When Julie Bortz was around, we would typically triple the chocolate chip cookie recipe. We figured one batch for the girls, one for the neighbors, and one for "testing" along the way. I'm surprised I am not bigger!

Emily McDermitt '87-'98

I began working at the Logan about four or five years ago. It was my first "real" job other than baby-sitting, so I was a little nervous at first. Now, I am very grateful because I've learned so much about myself, about our precious Lord, and about the hotel.

I have grown a lot in my faith, thanks to the morning Bible studies and walks to the beach, and I have overcome a lot of personal feelings, such as rejection. The Logan has the most peaceful and comforting atmosphere to me. Larry, Joyce, and the other workers are so gracious, compassionate, friendly, and understanding, and I will never forget the wonderful feelings we've experienced, stories we've shared, and memories we've made.

I have enjoyed helping the guests to have a good vacation and spending time with all the Loganettes. There are so many funny attic stories that I can't go through them all in such a short essay. One episode I will share, however, was the time when Jenny Parent, Sarah Wallington, and I scared Shannon Snow. Shannon was working late on desk, and we set up a fake person in her bed, wearing her clothes. I remember this well, because Sarah Busick took pictures of us! Anyway, when Shannon finished closing up the hotel, she came upstairs to see her surprise. Then we all laughed at the incident.

There are many other crazy memories, as well as many intimate discussions, that will always remain in our hearts. I am so blessed to have had the opportunity to share those times with special friends.

Jillian Volpe '95-'98

Chapter 25

Home on the "Range"

...and gives food to her household, and portions to her maidens (Proverbs 31:15).

Can you imagine sharing your kitchen with 35 teenagers over a four-month period? Our stove has produced a wide "range" of dishes over the years. Managers and chambermaids roll up their sleeves and pitch in at mealtimes. We have a chart of daily responsibilities always posted on the refrigerator. Cooking the evening meal brings out the creative juices in these aspiring "Proverbs 31" women who "range" in various degrees of experience when it comes to culinary arts. Many of them have had experience at home, while some of them are still in the "apprentice stage." In any event, mealtime is always an adventure!

We've enjoyed many wonderful meals as a result of their labors of love–not to mention lots of tempting, yummy desserts! This book could not contain the wonderful meals that have come from the Logan kitchen over the years. Just for fun, I thought I would share some of the most *unusual* dishes that the girls and I have produced over the years.

Rice for the Nations (anyone have any good rice recipes?)
Unidentifiable Chicken Parts (topic for "go around the table": "Name that nugget!")
Brownies Italiano (make with olive oil; serve with spaghetti)
Jell-O Juice (for those who can't seem to "firm up" their meal plans)
Jaw-Breaker Brownies (Larry: "Are these chocolate crumbs on my sledge hammer?")
Eat-and-"Run" Buns (bran muffins with nine times the baking soda)
Tubs of Subs (twicc as many subs were ordered by mistake, to the tune of $50)
Popped Charcoal (goes well with most videos, especially *Black Beauty*)
Scrambled Eggs a la Crunch (" 'Shell' We Gather at the River?")
Hamburger Nuggets (too small for buns)
UFOs (Unidentified Frozen Objects)
Shrink-Art Bacon Bits (new movie release: *Honey, I Shrunk the Breakfast*)
Mystery Meals (that make us think of manna–what is it?)
UFOs (Unidentified Furry Objects [from the back of the fridge]–sure to tickle your palate!)
Various Burnt Offerings (oh well, we can always send out for "tubs of subs"!)
Smashed Watermelon (is that what the Bible means by scattering our seed?)
Curds and Whey (too-old milk on cereal of your choice)
Cajun Casseroles (blackened to perfection)
"Hole Wheat" Bread (a "Weight Watchers" special)
Macaroni and Cheese Balls (now what did I do with the cheese sauce recipe?)

Golden Cholesterol Bake (sure to raise eyebrows as well as your cholesterol)
Surprise Stew (now what happened to that fly?)
Norwegian Meat Pudding (that even a Siberian Husky won't touch!)
Shaved Toast and Jelly (don't you just love eating at the "out-black"!)
Potatoes Ugh Rotten (unfortunately, self-explanatory)

If you find your mouth watering after reading this list of unusual delights, the Logan kitchen may consider take-out orders in the future.

All kidding aside, my girls are wonderful little cooks. Many of you have even gotten a whiff of their accomplishments. We continue to practice First Peter 4:9, which says, "Be hospitable to one another without complaint." On many occasions, we invite people to the infamous dining room table to join us for a meal. No matter how much experience they have had in the past, it doesn't take long before these Logan Ladies learn to feel at home on the "range."

"Dear Lord, what a privilege it is to take young people under our wing. There's no greater investment we could make than to invest in the lives of others. Thank You for investing in our lives, Lord, and for being so patient as we too learn by trial and error–in Jesus' name we pray, amen."

Memories From the Attic

One of the jobs of a chambermaid was to make dinner, so it came time to be my turn along with my friend Nancy. I wasn't worried since I cooked at home. All we had to do was cook chicken, rice, and some green beans. Well, the chicken was fine, so were the beans. But I wasn't too good with measurements, so the rice was another story. I looked at the box of rice, calculated how much we would need, and I thought that we needed more than one box for eight people. Three boxes later, Joyce walked in, and I told her that we needed more rice! She looked around and asked me, "How many boxes did you use?" After I showed her, she began to chuckle and asked me how I figured out the amount. I looked at the cups of uncooked rice as how many people would be served. Oops! That is how the Logan had rice all summer, or was it enough for two summers?

Denise G. Stang '85-'89,'92

Chapter 26

Heart Strings and Smiley Faces

... "Permit the children to come to Me; do not hinder them; for the kingdom of God belongs to such as these. Truly I say to you, whoever does not receive the kingdom of God like a child shall not enter it at all." And He took them in His arms and began blessing them, laying His hands upon them (Mark 10:14-16).

Some children have said things that still swing on the strings of my heart. Others have left indelible smiles. I'd like to devote this chapter to all those little people who have left precious fingerprints on the walls of my heart.

* * *

One little boy and his mother sat next to me in the lobby. "If you had one wish, Tommy, what would it be?" I asked, trying to get to know him better.

"I wish I could see my daddy," he replied. (I figured that his dad couldn't come because of work.)

"I wish I could see my daddy too," I said. "But he's up in Heaven."

Then, with a reply that still swings on the strings of my heart, he said sadly, "I don't know where my daddy is!"

* * *

Donovan's dad had passed away the previous year. Sitting on the steps that led to the second floor, I watched him and his older sister Chelsea play in the lobby. (We always keep a box of toys for the children behind the chair in the corner). Eventually, Donovan came over to sit beside me. He looked into my face with his sad blue eyes and said, "My daddy is dead, and I don't know if he is ever coming back!" My heart sank. Then with the amazing resilience of a three-year-old, he smiled, lifted one little foot into the air, and asked, "Did you see my new shoes?"

* * *

Kristi and her children invited me to join them for Happy Meals at McDonalds. Of course, I jumped at the chance to spend time with the grandchildren. As we munched our McNuggets, Rosemary, the five-year-old, spoke up. "Memaw, I fell off the water fountain today and hit my head." Before I could comment, her three-year-old brother's forehead was etched with concern. Anthony exclaimed, "Wosemawy, did you dwown?"

"No, silly, when you drown, you're dead!" Rosemary giggled.

Embarrassed, Anthony held up his little hands and shrugged his shoulders. He rolled his eyes up as if to say, "How would I know?" Slowly, a smile of relief changed his expression. He was relieved to know that he could look forward to more "happy meals" in the days to come.

* * *

I really miss my grandchildren in the summertime. Chip and Kristi try to bring them to the Logan as much as possible, but my heart wishes it would be more often. I do treasure the phone calls I receive with little voices on the other end asking to speak to Memaw!

Take Chip and Brenda's son, Miles, for instance. When he was five, he called me one afternoon. "Hi, Grandma," he said, "how are you feeling?"

"I'm fine, Miles, but I have a sore back."

"Are you taking pills about it?" he asked.

Later in the conversation, I asked him about the weather in Pennsylvania. "Oh, it's raining cats and buckets here," he said. Then speaking in a very grown-up voice he asked, "Is Granddad prepared to talk with me now?"

Miles is the one who, at the age of four, used to sit in his favorite chair and "think about life." He loved to lay on his back in the grass in his backyard, watching the clouds go by and ask questions like, "Mommy, are there stair steps that take us through those clouds and up to Heaven? What's the difference between God and Jesus? How long is 20 minutes?" (He also engages in conversation with people of all ages and then invites them over for dinner!)

If you were to ask this blonde-haired, brown-eyed little five-year-old what his favorite food was at that age, he would have said, "Gum." If questioned about his least favorite food, he would think for a moment and then say with a twinkle in his eye, "My least favorite is broccoli because it makes my hair turn upside down." "Miles" of smiles have come from this little one for sure.

* * *

Chip and Brenda's youngest son, Kirk, had just celebrated his second birthday in October. He and his mommy were Christmas shopping and stopped for lunch at McDonalds.

Kirk stuck three french fries in his catsup cup and sang at the top of his voice, “Happy birthday, dear Jesus, happy birthday to You!” He got a standing ovation by the workers, as well as all the patrons. (God even uses two-year-olds to remind us of the true meaning of Christmas.)

During the holidays, that same year, Larry and I had spent the night with Chip and his family. As Kirk and I sat in our pajamas holding hands, he lifted his little round face, looked me straight in the eye, and said, “So...Grandma...how are your fingernails doing?”

Kirk was up early one morning and was so hungry that I fixed him a bowl of cereal, sat him up to the breakfast bar, and asked him if he would like to pray. He said, “Grandma, take a seat!”

He prays these days with hands folded and one finger sticking out. He uses his high-pitched, reverent prayer voice and begins to pray so seriously, “Dear Jesus....” (It’s really hard to keep from laughing.) He points to everyone in the room and blesses them with his finger extended from his little praying hands. Then, he raises up in his high chair enough to point down at his plate and thanks God for each and every thing: “Thank You for my peas, thank You for my turkey, thank You for my applesauce.” Perhaps people like me who sometimes take things for granted can learn a lesson from such a grateful little heart.

* * *

Kristi was in the middle of her first year of teaching when Rosemary was born on February 29. She had to go back to work after six weeks to finish out the year, so I got the awesome privilege of taking care of my new granddaughter. It was so hard for Kristi to leave her firstborn that she got teary every morning as she left her in my arms. I remember walking around the house with Rosemary singing her to sleep. For some reason, "Silent Night" seemed to soothe her the most. Nine months later, we were all at a family group Christmas party (a home Bible study group we've belonged to for over 20 years). Rosemary was in her mommy's arms at the front of the room, and I was standing in the back. As we visited with our friends, Christmas carols played in the background. All of a sudden, "Silent Night" came over the P.A. system. Rosemary lifted her head from Kristi's shoulder and searched the room until her eyes met mine. Then she smiled at me as if to say, "Memaw, they are playing our song!"

* * *

Our friends, the Davises, adopted Teah when she was five years old. God, in His sovereignty, reached all the way across the whole world with loving arms and carried Teah from Korea to her new home in Rockville, Maryland. She looked like a little Oriental porcelain doll. Her sister Melissa and brother Jimmy enjoyed their new little sibling very much. Before long, Teah was willing to sleep on a real bed instead of the floor. She learned English very quickly and was soon ready to become an American citizen. When her mom and dad told Teah that they were going to take her to Baltimore to become Americanized, she got so excited. "Oh goody," she exclaimed, "can I have big blue ones like Jimmy's?"

* * *

A card from Alison, Kristi's middle child, has been a constant encouragement to me. It reads: "Remember the Holly One, He will see you throw!"

* * *

Right after Alison's great-grandfather died, she wrote a letter addressed to "JESUS in HEAVEN." After opening the homemade envelope, we read, "Dear Jesus, I love You. How is Grandad Mel doing? ________________ Love, Alison." (Don't we all wish that God would fill in the blanks?)

Another time, she said to me, "Memaw, sometimes when I sing songs to God, I get tears in my eyes!" (I believe that God is raising up a generation of children with hearts for worship!)

* * *

Several years ago, my friend Carol Clements was out running errands with her five-year-old grandson, Jeff. They stopped near a local retirement community to buy a few things at a grocery store. As they were leaving, Jeff, being quite observant, said, "Boy, there were a lot of old people in there!" On the way back to the car he asked, "Is Pop-Pop old? Grandma, are you old too?" After a brief discussion of the matter, they drove off down the road. Because it was the Easter season, Carol turned on the car radio to some sacred music. Jeff got a faraway look in his eyes. After a short period of speculation, he said, "You know what, Grandma? I think you were just little when Jesus was born."

* * *

In one of those serious moments, when my grandchildren's eyes were full of wonder, I said, "You know, kids, your great aunt Doris loves you very much! She thinks of you as her own grandchildren because she could never have any kids of her own." Looking very concerned, one of them said, "What happened, did she stand in front of the microwave?"

* * *

Three-year-old Rosemary was looking through some old picture albums with her family. Finding one of her mother (who looked very much like her at that age), she got very excited! Holding the picture up, she exclaimed, "When Mommy was little, she used to be me!"

* * *

Anthony was about four and a half when he sat on the deck with his great-grandfather watching the sunset. As the sun started descending behind the mountain, Granddad Mel said, "Look at the sun, Anthony. It will be gone pretty soon...going...going...going...gone!" Looking off into the distance, Anthony replied with a hushed voice, "Forever...!"

* * *

When our oldest grandson, Ben, was just a toddler, he was sent down the hall to his bedroom for a "time out." There was a long silence. He reappeared sheepishly riding toward us on his little tricycle. A halo of blond ringlets circled his head. He was so adorable that it was hard not to laugh. Looking very repentant, he lifted his blue eyes and said with a loud voice that echoed through the hallway, "Solllly...!"

One night, as we sat down to a Mexican dinner, Ben, who was about four at the time, looked at his dad and said with excitement, "We're having tacos, Daddy! Can I decorate my own?"

On another occasion I was telling little Benjamin the story about Samuel, paraphrasing from First Samuel 3 in a way that he could understand. I tried to make it as interesting as I could for this little four-year-old by putting a lot of inflection in my voice. "Samuel was spending the night with his friend Eli. God said, 'Saammuel...!' and Samuel jumped out of bed, ran to Eli, and said, 'What, Eli?' Then Eli said, 'It wasn't me. Go back to bed.' " I repeated it three times! Then, I told him, "One more time, God called, 'Saammuel!' Samuel went to Eli, and Eli said, 'It wasn't me, it was God...go back to bed and listen.' " After I finished telling the story, Ben sat quietly beside me looking very serious. Then, he said slowly, "G-r-a-n-d-m-aaaa...." Having no idea what he was up to, I responded, "What, Ben?" Then, with a sober face, he said, "It wasn't me...it was God!"

* * *

Picture the scene: Anthony and Larry (Anthony's hero), sitting on the couch in the family room. Larry picked up a walnut from the coffee table and cracked it open. He offered one to Anthony, who made a face and shook his head. "Don't you like walnuts?" Larry asked.

"No," he said.

"Well, do you like peanuts?"

"No."

"Do you like pecan nuts?"

"No," he said again. Not wanting to disappoint his grandfather, Anthony thought for a moment and then his face lit up as he said, "I like donuts!"

* * *

Two-year-old Melissa sat on Daddy's lap as he introduced her to her elbow. After a few moments of discovery, she straightened out her arm. With her green eyes filling with tears, she looked up into her Daddy's face. "Daddy, elbow's all gone, elbow's all gone!" she cried. (Elbows, like laps, may come and go, but isn't it great to know a Father's love that lasts forever?)

* * *

Christmas of 1998, I received two very special things written by my granddaughters that I wasted no time hanging on my *refrigerator*.

The first one was written by ten-year-old Rosemary. It is entitled "The Best Gift."

"The best gift I ever received is eternal life. I thank God for sending His Son down to die on the cross and sending Him to tell others about God. It is special because when I die, I will be spending my life in Heaven.

"The best gift I can give is friendship and kindness. I can give it to all of my friends and others even if they aren't kind to me. When you're about to say something unkind, think of a gift you can give instead."

The second piece was written by Alison, now nine. It was done on the computer, with a picture she constructed of a manger and a cross.

"Read Luke 2:20. See how the shepherds reacted when they had heard who was born. That is how we should react at Christ's birth too because God sent Him down here for a reason.

"Read John 3:16. That's how much God loves the world. We'd go to hell if it wasn't for Jesus coming to earth and dying for our sins. That is why we should be happy at His birth and death."

* * *

"Abba Father, we come as little children with outstretched arms saying, 'Hold me!' You take us into Your arms and hold us close to Your heart. We feel the warm sweet breath of Your Spirit on our necks as You softly whisper words of love and blessing...'My child, I've loved you so much that *I have inscribed you on the palms of My hands; your walls are continually before Me*' (Is. 49:16). It is exciting to think that we make lasting impressions on You, Lord. Do we leave fingerprints on the walls of Your heart as well? In Jesus' name we pray, amen."

Memories From the Attic

I was 19 years old, lonely, nervous, shy, and whining to God like a spoiled child. Now, suddenly, I was headed for a place I'd never been with people I had only just met. I was headed for my first summer at the Logan Hotel in Ocean City, New Jersey.

I am so thankful that God plucked me from my young world of insecurity and self-pity, and set me down in this quaint and cheerful haven among people who loved Him. As I learned the ins and outs of managing the hotel, God opened and exercised my latent gifts of teaching, serving, encouraging, and loving others. In this humble place, God also gently pried open my guarded heart and led me into beautiful friendships. In a setting that included faithful morning Bible studies, measured time for solitude, continual edification, and acceptance coupled with loving admonishment, God's grace also opened my eyes. He revealed to me an understanding of His holiness, a revelation that ceased the desire to complain, and He unleashed songs of praise and trust.

By God's hand, the Logan came into my life very much like a beacon comes into the life of a sailor lost at sea by calling one in from the dark, lonely oceans of the world and into the marvels of God's grace.

Sharon (Buysee) Griffith '88-'90

Chapter 27

Ruth and Boaz

Thy word is a lamp to my feet, and a light to my path (Psalm 119:105).

Have you ever been accused of being overprotective parents? We have—on many occasions! After raising two kids of our own, we've become very good at it. Having the responsibility of 35 beautiful teenage girls each summer has almost made us experts! From time to time, Larry and I sit down and discuss the matter. Are we too strict? Should we loosen the reins? Are we being too overprotective? Each time, we hear a resounding "No!" After all, we are responsible for the safety of these precious maidens!

When the new aspiring chambermaids come to the orientation meetings, the rules are discussed in front of their parents. A contract is signed by each girl in which each promises to abide by a whole list of rules, including not speaking to strangers, wearing modest clothing, and having attitudes that would glorify Jesus. If they meet someone at a Christian gathering and want to date him, it has to meet with their parents' approval as well as ours.

Perhaps this will paint a backdrop for the story I'm going to share with you.

Each year we earnestly pray for the new staff. We don't want the "harvest to be too great and the workers to be too few." Recruiting is a prayerful and painful process, but this particular spring, we were all set!

One day a friend called and said she knew a 19-year-old girl named Sharon who would make an excellent manager. I don't usually take someone sight unseen. After discussing the matter, however, Larry felt impressed to hire her. I agreed even though it didn't seem practical. We were already fully staffed, but it was God's decision, and He always makes good ones.

I remember the day Sharon's mom dropped her off. She seemed very shy as she peered at us through the long, blonde hair that covered half her face.

We trusted our friend's recommendation and God's guidance, but we wondered how things would work out. "Will she feel comfortable with us? How will she interact with the other girls?" I wondered what God was going to do.

Well, as it turned out, Sharon was a gem. She caught onto the managerial duties quickly. Her attitude was great. She embraced the younger girls like little sisters. She still sends some of them birthday cards to this day! The thing that impressed and convicted me at the same time was her love for God. During her times off, when the other girls were at the beach, I would see her sitting at the table on the side porch. With head bowed for sometimes an hour or more, she prayed. Not only did we get a manager, but we also got an intercessor!

On the first Memorial Day weekend that Sharon was at the Logan, we decided to invite people over to play Pictionary. It's a game that is similar to charades, but instead of acting, you have to call on your artistic abilities (whether you have any or not). It's a lot of fun. Anyway, among the invited guests was Gary Griffith, our lawyer friend in Ocean City. That was only the beginning!

Gary was quite a few years older than Sharon. His increasing interest in her caused a growing concern in this overprotective, substitute-mother's heart. I was so concerned that I told Sharon that I suspected that Gary was "smitten" (as if she didn't already know). I was unsure of her feelings about the matter, for she just silently stared at me with those big blue eyes of hers.

Maybe we should call her mother! I said to myself, waiting to pray more about it. That night as I crawled into bed and started to talk to God about the situation, I felt impressed to pick up my Bible. Turning "at random" to the Book of Ruth, my eyes fell on a footnote that brought everything into focus. Boaz was much older than Ruth, and God had been the matchmaker! I closed my Bible, turned out the light, and pulled up the covers. How nice it was to peacefully sleep in the arms of my sovereign Lord.

"Dear Wonderful Counselor, thank You for giving us *rhema* (the quickened Word of God) that jumps off the page and speaks personally to our hearts. You go before us and have great plans that we have only yet to discover. How exciting it is to see them unfold as we trust You each step of the way. Thank You for being such a protective Parent! In Jesus' name we pray, amen."

I will bless the Lord who has counseled me; indeed, my mind instructs me in the night (Psalm 16:7).

Man shall not live on bread alone, but on every [rhema] *word that proceeds out of the mouth of God* (Matthew 4:4b).

* * *

Update!

Gary and Sharon married two years later with the blessing of both sets of parents. They deeply love the Lord and one another. Presently, they live in Ocean City with their three daughters, Sam, Joy, and Mercy, and they continue to be a blessing to these "overprotective parents" at the Logan!

Memories From the Attic

I don't really know how it happened. We wound up on the same team in a Pictionary game at the Logan almost 11 years ago...and now we are married with three sprightly daughters.

I met Gary on my third day at the Logan. It was Memorial Day weekend, and he came by to see the Coffins. I had just returned from an errand to the supermarket. Joyce introduced us and then realized that she had forgotten to ask me to buy eggs and milk. Gary offered to drive me. Telling the story now, he says that I didn't say one word on the trip to and from the store.

Gary, a friend of Larry and Joyce through his best friend Robby, often visited the Logan, especially for Saturday night sing-alongs. Gary was like no other person I had met. He was full of confidence, humor (although harsh humor at times), and direction. Within the week following our first meeting, Gary and I were teamed with Joyce in the fateful Pictionary game. At that time, I couldn't remember ever having laughed more. From then on, the summer was filled with early morning bicycle trips to deliver jars of juice to his doorstep (he had no food in his kitchen), late nights watching the Yankees together, and hours of fun conversation around the Logan table.

God's timing and matchmaking are perfect. Gary often says, "Everything Sharon likes to do and is good at, I can't do, and everything I like to do and am good at, Sharon doesn't enjoy doing."

We still live in Ocean City, and our girls love to visit the Logan to see Larry and Joyce and our friends who work there. Our little ones often ask Daddy to tell the story of how we met, and he loves to indulge them with the details again and again.

Sharon (Buysee) Griffith '88-'90

Chapter 28

Wisdom at My Disposal

But if we walk in the light as He Himself is in the light, we have fellowship with one another, and the blood of Jesus His Son cleanses us from all sin (1 John 1:7).

I love it when God teaches us spiritual lessons through things in the natural. Dirty dishes were stacked so high that I could hardly find the sink (which seemed to be calling my name in muffled tones somewhere beneath the debris). Many hindrances had kept me from "looking well to the ways of my household" (see Prov. 31:27). Purposing to no longer procrastinate, I cleared a path to the faucet and proceeded with the task at hand. Running the hot water full force, I desperately tried to scrape away the hardened food deposits. Before long, I noticed the water backing up in the sink!

"Oh, no," was my first reaction. "All I need now is a plumbing problem!"

All of a sudden, things went from bad to worse—smelly garbage started to float to the surface! Vaguely familiar globs started raising their ugly heads! From the looks of things I hadn't run my garbage disposal for at least two days! How could I have been so neglectful? (As always, with the revelation came the remedy.) I flipped the switch. What a relief it was to see that whirlpool of water whisking away every trace of evidence.

Above the roar of the disposal, these words of wisdom were impressed on my heart. "This is like your spiritual life. My living water cannot flow freely through clogged pipes. It's very important that you constantly run your 'garbage disposal' by confessing your sins to Me. If you don't, the 'garbage' will collect and (when you least expect it) will float to the surface for all to see!"

"Dear Lord, as we run our spiritual garbage disposals, wash away every trace of sin. We want Your living water to flow unhindered through our lives. Please deliver us from the perils of procrastination, especially where You are concerned. In Jesus' name we pray, amen."

If we confess our sins, He is faithful and righteous to forgive us our sins and to cleanse us from all unrighteousness (1 John 1:9).

Memories From the Attic

Working at the Logan was not just a mere job; it was an experience. When I think about my time there, I don't just think about the "joberdos" and cleaning the rooms. Instead, my fondest memories are of the early morning Bible studies I attended, the friends I made, and the wonderful people I met and got a chance to serve. I can honestly say that my time and experience at the Logan truly changed my life.

Even before I was officially a Loganette, I remember Joyce letting me dust the baseboards and do odd jobs while my parents, the Davises, helped open the Logan every spring. I literally grew up with the Logan. When I "became of age," I was allowed to be a chambermaid, and even more exciting to me at that time was that I would get to sleep in the attic with the "big girls." From that first weekend as a chambermaid, I grew, and I finally made my way to being a manager for the whole summer.

Working at the Logan gave me the chance to make mistakes, and boy, did I make my share, but it also allowed me to learn a lot about my relationship with God. Every morning I was given the opportunity to grow closer to God by experiencing the beauty and amazement of His love through nature and His Word.

Now when I go back as a guest, I can experience that feeling the guests told me about. You really do feel welcome and you can feel the Lord's presence and His happiness.

Teah (Davis) DeVan '87-'93

What a wonderful preparation for so many things...

- *Motherhood through managing over younger chambermaids, "proper and thorough cleaning."*

- *Diligent and regular prayer time and study. Evidence of answered prayer as our list of prayer needs were met!*
- *Joyce and Larry didn't always have "help" lined up for some weeks, but God rewarded their faith and always provided the needed managers and chambermaids.*
- *Humor was the backbone of the mealtimes, beach times, and sing-alongs, which made the Logan such a special place to work.*

Rory (Gehman) Kolb '90

Chapter 29

Grasshoppers and Giants

...and we became like grasshoppers in our own sight... (Numbers 13:33).

Have you ever felt like a grasshopper? I have. Do you remember the story in Numbers 13 when Moses sent spies into the land of Canaan? They went to "see what the land is like, and whether the people who live in it are strong or weak, whether they are few or many" (Num. 13:18). The spies came back after 40 days with two reports. One group reported that the land was "flowing with milk and honey," but they also said that the people were strong, the cities were fortified, and there where giants in the land! They said that they "became like grasshoppers" in their sight (see Num. 13:27-33). Another reporter, Caleb, was optimistic. He said, "We should by all means go up and take possession of it, for we shall surely overcome it" (Num. 13:30b). Caleb and Joshua told the people that the Lord would bring them into the land and give it to them. They reassured them that the protection over the giants had been removed and that the Israelites needn't fear (see Num. 14:9). Their optimistic attitudes caused an uproar. Which side of the fence would you and I have been on?

Well, there was one night at the Logan when I looked in my mirror and all I could see was a weak little grasshopper staring back at me!... Let me tell you the rest of the story.

When the two girls checked in, I was a little suspicious. They agreed to the rules about no drinking, etc., but I had my reservations. Rebellion glared at me through thick black mascara. (Since that time, we've learned to say that we cater to older people and families and that younger adult guests really wouldn't have any fun here.) This time, I had to trust their word when they agreed to follow our rules (at least for the time being). (We try to keep our rates low so that people can afford to come, but sometimes that works against us. It seems to attract people who will promise anything just to pay the cheaper rate.) Trusting God to protect us, I showed them up to their room.

Increasing uneasiness made it hard to fall asleep that night. I had given the girls a key to the front door, as I do all the other guests, but I had no way of knowing what the night would bring. After dozing off, I was awakened by boisterous laughing and the sound of people stumbling up the steps. (Our Room 5 is partially under the stairway.) Quickly putting on my robe, I went into the hallway. There was a momentary silence as they went into Room 6 and closed the door. I waited and listened. After a few seconds, noise, louder than ever, reverberated throughout the silent hallways.

"They must be drunk!" I said. "Lord, I really need You this time!" I whispered under my breath.

Now I am not petite by any stretch of the imagination. But passing by the full length mirror in the hall, this 5'5", size 14, woman of faith "became as a grasshopper" in her own sight! It's amazing how circumstances can change one's perspective. It was no coincidence that I had just read that account of giants and grasshoppers in my quiet time. I prayed to the Lord for the courage of Caleb as I climbed the stairs to the second floor. My faith increased with every step. By the time I got to their door, I was a grasshopper no more! I knocked quietly so that I wouldn't disturb the other guests; I waited for them to open it so I could speak to them face to face. "Girls, I know you have been drinking," I said sternly. "Because you have broken the Logan rules, you'll have to find another place to stay." And then as my new-found boldness became tempered with mercy, I said, "I'll give you permission to stay the rest of the night if you quietly go to bed, and I'll give you your money back for the rest of your stay if you don't cause any more trouble." They sheepishly agreed and quietly closed their door.

I went back down the steps, turned the corner by the front desk, and glanced into that mirror in the hall, only to discover that I wasn't a grasshopper after all!

As I went into my room, I hung up my robe and crawled into bed. This time, I went right to sleep. (As for Room 6, there wasn't another peep.)

"Dear heavenly Father, every time we grasshoppers take a leap of faith, You are there to catch us. When those giant-sized problems rise up before us, help us to know that the battle isn't ours, but Yours (see 1 Sam. 17:47b). In Jesus' name we pray, amen."

And we urge you, brethren, admonish the unruly, encourage the fainthearted, help the weak, be patient with all men (1 Thessalonians 5:14).

Memories From the Attic

"Give ear to my words, O Lord, consider my meditation. Give heed to the voice of my cry, my King and my God, for to You I will pray. My voice You shall hear in the morning, O Lord; in the morning I will direct it to You, and I will look up" (Ps. 5:1-3 NKJ). Each day at the Logan started with times of devotion, group prayer, putting on the armor of God, Bible studies, and personal quiet times. My eyes were opened to a whole new realm of praise. I learned that I come before the Lord not because of the righteous things I have done, but because of His mercy (see Ps. 5:7-8 NKJ). I was challenged to focus prayer on worshiping the Lord and to praise Him for who He is and His mighty acts: "Who is like You, glorious in holiness, fearful in praises, doing wonders?" (Ex. 15:11b NKJ) By praising Him, I glorify Him (see Ps. 50:23 NKJ). Because of the depth of the riches of the Lord's wisdom and knowledge, there is no limit to what I can learn of Him (see Rom. 11:33-36 NKJ). Two Bible study topics remain vivid to me. One was of the Lord's covenantal relationship to man and of the significance of His actions and words when cutting His covenant with Abraham (see Gen. 15). This redeeming, everlasting faithfulness is life-transforming! The other looked at the Lord's Hebrew names. By learning the meaning behind each name, I was shown new glimpses of the Lord's character and being. The Lord used these gems to reveal more and more of Himself to me. I thank and praise Him for this priceless gift.

Patricia Rice '90-'98

Chapter 30

The Strong Tower

The name of the Lord is a strong tower; the righteous runs into it and is safe (Proverbs 18:10).

What a blessing it is to hear my girls pray with the Hebrew names of God. At 7:00 each morning, the girls and I gather for prayer and Bible study around the dining room table. After quietly singing a few songs of praise, we open with prayer. "[Come] magnify the Lord with me," I often say, "and let us exalt His name together" (Ps. 34:3). Many times I hold up a giant magnifying glass and remind them that we can't hold it on the Lord and ourselves at the same time. Neither can we look at Him and magnify our problems. That old magnifying glass makes a great visual aid, one that I even use on myself from time to time.

Kay Arthur's book, *Lord, I Want to Know You*, is a wonderful study on the Hebrew names of God. In Bible times, a name described a person's character. This study of the meanings of God's names has done more for me than any other in helping me to grow to know Him in a more intimate way. When we know Him, we can't help but love Him. He is like a many-faceted diamond reflecting His wonderful nature to all those who seek Him. I love to share His names with my girls. I wait to see them grab hold of ones that impress them the most. Then before long, they too begin to use His Hebrew names in prayer.

As I reflect on His names, I become mindful of the ways God has been there for us since that first day when we stepped across the Logan threshold and became innkeepers. As I get older, I've learned to appreciate His involvement in my life even more. Running the Logan has helped me to see Him in a new light.

Elohim–Our Creator. (The first mention of this name is in Genesis 1:1.) God, my Creator, taught me that I was a one-of-a-kind original. I am "accepted in the beloved" (see Eph. 1:6 KJV). I no longer have to compare myself with anyone else. I worship Him as my Elohim every time I go up the back stairs to close the doors at night and see those spectacular sunsets. I stand in awe of Elohim as I watch the waves crashing on the shore. I marvel at His creativity when I look at the uniqueness of each one of my girls and observe the variety of people on the boardwalk. I bask in His goodness as I review the registration cards from past years and think of the many wonderful people who have passed through the revolving doors of my heart. Each person has left lasting footprints, and no two are the same. Elohim is so great. His creativity sometimes leaves me speechless.

El Elyon–The Most High God. (See Genesis 14:18-20.) This name has been so meaningful in my life. I run into the strong tower of His sovereignty and find safety in the knowledge that He is always in control. He was in control of my life even when I failed to acknowledge the fact. He was in control all the times I was learning by trial and error. He was in control even when things looked out of control. When evil seems to have the upper hand, He is always higher still. He is the Most High God. I lift my eyes to worship Him, for I am so grateful.

El Roi—The God Who Sees. (See Genesis 16:13 and Psalm 139:7-12.) Just as God saw Hagar in the wilderness, He saw me—languishing in loneliness, drowning in the depths of despair, crying in the showers, tossing in my bed, praying passionately for wisdom, fearing fear itself, being anxious over all kinds of things time and time again. He not only sees, but He makes provision.

El Shaddai—The All-Sufficient One. (See Genesis 17:1-8.) This name brings to mind a nursing mother hovering over her child. The word *shad* means breast. I don't mean to say that He is female by any stretch of the imagination, but God does nurture His children. Just as a baby looks to its mother for its life, we look to El Shaddai, and when we do, He pours out His blessings and righteous judgments that are so much more merciful than our own. When it comes right down to it, He is all we need. El Shaddai is life itself!

Adonai—The Lord. (See Genesis 15:2.) You can recognize Adonai in our Bibles by capital "L," lowercase "ord." (All-caps LORD is used to represent *Jehovah.*) Accepting Jesus as my Lord the first summer we had the Logan was the best "move" I ever made. (I moved off the throne of my life to make room for Him.) I didn't know His name was Adonai at the time. I only knew that I was making a mess of things on my own. Giving up the reins meant consulting Him on decisions, asking Him for direction, denying self, picking up the cross, and following Him no matter where He chose to lead me (see Mt. 16:24). I think it's a good idea for us to ask Him if there is any area in our lives that is not under His loving Lordship. Adonai will answer. I know from experience!

Jehovah Jireh—The Lord Is Our Provider. (See Genesis 22:14.) God the Father provided the best gift of all in His Son. Jesus is our provision. He is "the way, and the truth, and the life" (see Jn. 14:6). No one comes to the Father, but by Him. He also opens His hand and satisfies the desire of every living thing (see Ps. 145:16). He has provided the finances to run the Logan and pay all our expenses. His "staff" has comforted us for 27 years. He has given us the strength and encouragement that we have needed each day. He has given us wisdom every time we have prayed as Jehoshaphat prayed, "We do not know what to do, but our eyes are upon You" (2 Chron. 20:12b NIV). He has provided us with reliable vans to shuttle the kids back and forth from Maryland to New Jersey all these years. He has provided us with daily bread and more! He has opened up His Word to us in new and exciting ways, engraving His truths forever on our hearts. He has sent wonderful guests. He provides the protection we need. He continues to keep our light burning even when the powers of darkness try to snuff it out. We praise You, Jehovah Jireh, for providing Your Son and Your ongoing provision.

Jehovah Rapha—The Lord Who Heals. (See Exodus 15:26.) God comes with "healing" in His "wings" even today (see Mal. 4:2). I have been healed of deafness in my left ear, car sickness, eye infections, and many other things. There still remains a mystery about physical healing. I don't know why some things are healed and some things are not. "The secret things belong to the Lord our God, but the things revealed belong to us and to our children forever" (Deut. 29:29a NIV). I do know without a doubt, though, that God heals the brokenhearted. I've experienced emotional, mental, and spiritual healing in my own life (and witnessed it in others as well). I've done some biblical counseling. It is so exciting to meet people who really want Him to heal their broken hearts. I know that sounds strange, but some people really aren't ready yet for His healing. (By that, I mean that they come for sympathy and a listening ear, but they are not willing to do what God calls them to do to get better.) But the ones who have white-knuckled His faithfulness, obeyed His Word, and trusted Him are still walking in good health spiritually and emotionally to this day. (This is not to discount the fact that some people have to take medication for special needs, but some have been told by their doctors that they no longer need it!) Jehovah Rapha never ceases to amaze me! He will let us know about those "secret things" that we don't understand–in His time.

Jehovah Sabaoth–The Lord of Hosts. (See First Samuel 1:1-3.) This is the name that we cry out in our extremity. Remember Hannah, who cried out to the Lord of Hosts in her barrenness. When David fought the giant, he bravely went forward in the name of Jehovah Sabaoth. Do you ever feel like you are at the end of your rope of ability and strength? I have felt that way on many occasions–like the time I felt as though I couldn't manage being an innkeeper; like the time I tried to wear too many hats and they kept falling off; like the time the furnace spewed black smoke and the fire alarms kept going off for no reason; like the time I needed to dispense discipline and my "dispenser" was clogged with fear; and like the many times I had to turn away people who didn't like our rules. The list goes on and on. But so does the help of our Jehovah Sabaoth! The next time you get to the end of your rope, hang on, say a prayer, and the Lord of Hosts will meet you there.

Jehovah Shalom–The Lord Is Peace. (See Judges 6:24.) I can identify with Gideon when God gave him an overwhelming job to do. Can't you? It's wonderful that peace is one of our fringe benefits. I've met Jehovah Shalom many times in my life. He rode in the ambulance with me when I miscarried our first baby and almost bled to death. He met me on the beach when I put Larry and the children on the altar of His love. He remained my peace when the future seemed uncertain. He rode on the stretcher with me as I was wheeled into brain tumor surgery. He rode with us through every storm that came up the coast. He gave us that peace that surpasses all understanding to enable us to stay in business even when the staff outnumbered the guests (see Phil. 4:7 NKJ). I praise my Prince of Peace who gives "perfect peace" as my "mind is stayed on Him" (see Is. 26:3 KJV).

Jehovah Raah–The Lord Is My Shepherd. (See Psalm 23:1.) This name is one that is the most familiar to folks. It is the most popular Scripture at funerals. Years ago, I heard a tape by Bob Mumford who referred to Psalm 23 as a "psalm for the living." He manifests Himself as our Good Shepherd every day. Jehovah Raah leads us and guides us, feeds us and hides us. He loves us so much that He laid down His life for His sheep (see Jn. 10:11). I'm learning to enjoy His still waters in the midst of turmoil, His green pastures in the midst of unrest, His restoration when I become undone, and His paths of righteousness when I lose my way. His presence illumines my dark valleys. His faith dispels fear. I've learned to appreciate the comfort of His rod of authority and His staff of guidance. His table is solidly set in the midst of our enemies, and it is the anointing of the oil of His Spirit that overflows my cup. It is His goodness and lovingkindness that will indeed follow me all the days of my life. (See Psalm 23.)

The Lord is my wonderful Shepherd. In light of who He is, I should never want again!

Jehovah Tsidkenu–The Lord Our Righteousness. (See Jeremiah 23:6.) One morning I asked the girls to raise their hands if they were righteous. Very few hands went up. Most people measure righteousness by good works. The Scripture says that our righteousness is as "filthy rags" (see Is. 64:6 KJV). And we at the Logan, of all people, know about filthy rags! The bottom line is, no one is righteous apart from Him. Remember the story of the prodigal son? The father didn't hesitate to embrace his rag-clad kid. Our Father races to replace our rags with His robe of righteousness. When we return to Him, He invites the angels to a party given on our behalf. In light of that truth, all our hands should go up when we are asked, "Who is righteous?" And it is not because of us, but because of Jesus who shed His blood to make it happen. When God looks down, He sees a spotless lamb. Praise God! He did the work, and we get the robe!

A whole book could be written on each of God's names. This is just a sampling of some that have become dear to our hearts here at the Logan. (Maybe it will whet your appetite to study the Hebrew names of God yourself.) In the meantime, I invite you to come "magnify the Lord with me, and let us exalt His name together" (Ps. 34:3). The rewards are great! Remember, "The name of the Lord is a strong tower; the *righteous* runs into it and is safe" (Prov. 18:10). See you there! He's as close as a prayer.

"Dear Lord Jesus, we desire to know You in a more intimate way. Help us to put all our confidence in the name of the Lord our God. As we curl up in Your cozy robe of righteousness, it's so comforting to know where we can run in the time of trouble. In Your holy name we pray, amen."

Memories From the Attic

I worked at the Logan for eight years, and you would think that after all that time I'd be able to sit down and whip up a short memoir of a particular person, event, or lesson learned in no time. You would think...but it's not easy at all. In fact, it's just about impossible. There are far too many significant people, events, and lessons learned to choose just one. I can only tell you that the Logan is one of my favorite places in the world. I made and cemented friendships there that will continue throughout my life. I watched God work miracles in the lives of guests and friends, and I experienced His hand in my own life as I received the spiritual training and guidance that helped my young faith to mature. I praise the Lord for the time He gave me to laugh, learn, and clean at the Logan. I will cherish those memories and draw on that spiritual foundation for the rest of my life.

Kristen Parent '91-'98

A few things I remember about my summers at the Logan:

- *Joyce making pancakes in the shape of animals for the guests' children during a hurricane.*
- *Trying to lug around "Big Mama" (the industrial-sized vacuum cleaner).*
- *Room 5 and "Room 5 Talks"*
- *Joyce teaching me how to jitterbug in the lobby.*

Teah (Davis) DeVan '87-'93

Chapter 31

Noel's Story

Even though I walk through the valley of the shadow of death, I fear no evil (Psalm 23:4a).

I often refer to my Logan girls as angels, although I was unaware that one would one day be knocking on Heaven's door within hours after saying good-bye!

Father's Day fell on the twentieth of June in the summer of 1993. The van headed back to Maryland that day filled with excited chambermaids who were looking forward to seeing their dads. Noel (one of the three McDermitt girls who has worked for us), was dropped off at her home in Olney, Maryland. After spending time with her family, she drove over to a friend's house nearby for a short visit. Then on her way back home she was broadsided by a speeding car as she crossed an intersection on Georgia Avenue, three blocks from her house. Noel's neck was broken on impact. Like a lifeless little rag doll, she lay motionless with her head thrown back on her shoulders.

Thank God, a former fire chief and paramedic *just so happened* to be in the intersection at the time. He jumped out of his car and ran to her aid. Seeing that Noel had already started turning blue, he reached into the car and held her head upright to free her airway until the ambulance came. Because of the severity of her injuries, Noel was flown by helicopter to the University of Maryland's Shock Trauma Unit in Baltimore, where medical teams worked into the night to save her life. Time seemed to stand still for her family as she wavered between life and death. A "halo" (brace) was screwed into her skull to prevent further injury.

Back at the Logan, I was unaware that Noel was in such serious trouble. I had waved to the girls as they drove off that afternoon, never suspecting that within a few hours a wave of events would bring one of my precious girls so close to death.

That evening, I was in the lobby when the phone rang. It was Emily, Noel's older sister. Somehow, I sensed something was wrong. Then she told me, "Joyce, I called to tell you that Noel has been in a terrible accident. The doctors don't know if she will live through the night." I hung on every word as Emily continued, "I am here alone with the younger children. Mom and Dad left immediately to go be with Noel at the hospital. As soon as the lady came to the door to tell us what happened, I ran upstairs to get my Bible. I opened it to a verse that instantly gave me peace. It's from Psalm 21:4-7, 'He asked life of Thee, Thou didst give it to him, length of days forever and ever....and through the lovingkindness of the Most High he will not be shaken.' Joyce, El Elyon, our Most High God, is in control. I know she will be all right."

"God is in control. You are right, Emily!" I said, trying to hold back my tears. "Thanks so much for letting us know. The girls and I will be praying. Please keep us updated if you can. We love you, honey. Remember that God is faithful!"

Hanging up the phone, I was still in shock. I recalled studying the Hebrew names of God with the McDermitt girls on more than one occasion. Emily, the oldest of the three, had worked for us for several years by then and had hidden His names in her heart. God's Word had become her security during this time of trouble. Proverbs 18:10 says, "The name of the Lord is a strong tower; the righteous runs into it and is safe." Robed in His righteousness alone, we have the privilege of running into the high tower of His name, the "Most High God" (who is always in control) and find solace there.

I've always admired the McDermitt family's love for God. Their deep abiding faith saw them through Noel's long recovery. Her mom, Linda, stayed and prayed by her bedside day and night keeping vigil over her precious daughter.

Noel was impacted greatly by the accident. She loves to tell how God brought her through and used it to teach her valuable lessons.

A little comic relief is always welcomed in the midst of heartaches. When Noel woke up from her coma soon after the accident, she spoke with an English accent! A couple of days later, her dad, Mike, was watching the evening news. They were featuring head trauma (of all things), which sometimes results in a rare condition called Foreign Accent Syndrome. They interviewed a man who had started speaking with a German accent after hitting his head. Mike taped the show. Following the news clip, Mike then videotaped Noel in her "halo," sitting in the ICU, thanking everyone for their prayers with an English accent that was unmistakable. Her mom, after witnessing it for days, verified that it really was legitimate.

At the end of the summer, my little angel, Noel, complete with "halo," was well enough to come to the Logan for a short visit. She said that her experience gave her a deeper compassion for disabled people after taking a walk down the boardwalk in the midst of the stares and jeers. We sat in the lobby that evening and watched the "infamous" video. I continued to be amazed by Noel's story.

The "halo" came off October 5 of that year. The accent gradually wore off, but Noel's gratitude to her Most High God for getting her through never has abated. Outside of a little scar on her eyebrow, one would never know that she came so close to really "going Home" on Father's Day.

* * *

In closing, I would like to share with you a little poem I wrote for Noel while she was still in the ICU.

"After-Glow"

How do angels get their halos? Did you ever want to know?
Are they issued with the outfit, or do they have to grow?
Are they Heavenly rewards?...Do they have to fit just so?
How do angels get their halos? Did you ever want to know?
There once was an angel, who knocked on Heaven's door.
God's answer came, "Not yet, My love...for you, I've planned much more.
"Go back and tell them of My Son, I'll give you the words to say...
"You see, some people don't believe miracles are for today!
"You'll be supplied with grace, and patience to endure.
"Eye has not seen, and ear has not heard, all that I have in store!" (see 1 Cor. 2:9)

So the medics entertained an angel unaware (see Heb. 13:2),
As they daily met your needs with tender loving care.
When they placed the "halo" on your head, I bet they had no clue,
That the special glow that filled the room,
Was the light of Christ in you.

"O Most High God, we never know what each day will bring. When trouble comes crashing into our lives, we find safety in the strong tower of Your name. You are ever present at our crossroads of calamity. You reach into our brokenness and become the 'lifter of our heads' when we become too weak to hold them up on our own (see Ps. 3:3). Your breath gives us life. Your loving vigil sustains us through long nights of testing. What in the world would we do without You? In Jesus' name we pray, amen."

Memories From the Attic

They say that the longest distance for spiritual truths to travel is between your head and your heart. The Logan is where God's Word first became implanted upon my heart. It was there that I learned the importance of digging deep in the Scriptures and praying that the Lord would give me a ***rhema*** *word. That is how my love life with the Lord took off. I also encountered God's love in action, at the Logan, and learned the joy of serving others and of pleasing the Lord. The Logan was my launching pad in so many ways and I will always cherish my fond memories.*

Elena (Rice) Regitz '93-'98

The Logan

I learned so
much at this hotel
Well beyond how to
Clean rooms and showers
Rather, to clean my heart
For His stay
Day after day.

Karin Rice '91-'95

Chapter 32

Balloons for Daddy

Blessed be the God and Father of our Lord Jesus Christ, the Father of mercies and God of all comfort; who comforts us in all our affliction so that we may be able to comfort those who are in any affliction with the comfort with which we ourselves are comforted by God (2 Corinthians 1:3-4).

Jeff Varney always held a special place in our hearts. He was a very special young man, even as a teenager. We first met him when he came to the junior high youth group at the church where Larry and I volunteered as youth counselors. What a surprise it was to bump into Jeff on the boardwalk several years later in Ocean City, New Jersey, during the Youth for Christ week. Over a bowl of ice cream, he told us that he had moved to Virginia, became a high school teacher, and had eventually become a guidance counselor. It was wonderful to get reacquainted with him and to see how he was serving God in his life. A few years later, Jeff started to rent an apartment every June. He brought his wife Suzie and their two young children, Chelsea and Donovan.

A couple of summers ago, Jeff offered his help for the following spring. He was aware of how much work went into running the Logan and felt a desire to pitch in. We were touched by his offer. However, it never materialized. You see, that fall this precious man of God was found dead in his shower by little Chelsea. We came home from the Logan in September to receive the shocking answering machine message of his mysterious death. It remains a mystery.

The story I'm about to share is an episode that took place when Suzie brought the children back to the Logan for their annual visit–this time, without Daddy....

Suzie showed incredible strength as she leaned hard on God following her husband's unexplainable death. She and the children decided to return to their *favorite vacation spot* at the Logan, even though Daddy was now in Heaven. Revisiting familiar places is very hard after the passing of a loved one. Some people never do.

The day after they arrived happened to be Father's Day. I was concerned about how she and the little ones would handle this difficult holiday. And, I wondered why the young mother was so determined to find helium balloons that first morning. At the end of the day, we got the rest of the story.

"Did you find the balloons?" I asked when Suzie came up to the lobby.

"Yes, we went to the boardwalk and found smiley faced ones!" she answered. "I had brought magic markers from home so the children could draw pictures and write their love letters to Daddy on the balloons. When they finished, we walked hand in hand to the end of the jetty."

As she spoke, everyone within hearing distance began wiping their eyes. We could just picture the scene in our minds as Suzie described how they let go of the strings and watched as the two smiley faced messengers soared their way up *to Heaven.*

She could tell that her love mission was successful when she tucked her little ones into bed that night.

Smiles were so refreshing after such a season of tears.

"Dear Lord Jesus, our God of all comfort, only You can put smiles on broken hearts. After we go through our valleys of tears, enable us to be able to soar once more (see Ps. 84:6)! In Jesus' name we pray, amen."

* * *

Update!

Chelsea stopped singing in the children's choir at church after her daddy's death. Now, three years later, she looks forward to performing in a musical production near her home in Virginia. In the process of binding up her little broken heart, God has given her a new song to sing.

Memories From the Attic

In the summer before my freshman year of high school, my friend Alissa and I had the opportunity to work at the Logan as chambermaids. We were nervous as we rode up in the van with Larry to Ocean City, New Jersey, but the nervousness quickly wore off as we got to know Joyce and Larry, the other girls, and what the Logan was all about. God directed me to the Logan that summer because I was so far from Him. I was never a "bad" kid, as we would say, but I was hanging out with the wrong crowd and doing things I had no business doing. But I thought, "I am a Christian," and I believed that was enough. I had grown up in a Christian school and home, had already asked Jesus into my heart, and had many experiences in learning about God and being a Christian. I'd had my moments with God, but it wasn't until that summer that the Lord spoke to my heart saying I needed to take Him and my relationship with Him more seriously. My life would definitely be different had the Lord not led me to the Logan that first summer. I've made lasting friendships with many girls I've worked with at the Logan, and I have many fond memories of being there.

My heart smiles when I see pictures or things that remind me of the Logan. Joyce and Larry are like grandparents to me. I love them dearly. I can't wait until next summer!

Monica Tigert '96-'98

Chapter 33

Who Darkens My Door? Deliver Us From Evil

The Lord is my light and my salvation; whom shall I fear? The Lord is the defense of my life; whom shall I dread? (Psalm 27:1)

It was a voice that sent shivers down my spine. The only way I can describe it is witch-like. She called several times a week to ask if we had a room available. Sounds of passing cars whizzing by could be heard in the background.

"Hello, do you have any rooms?" she would screech. Now, as a Christian, I knew that lying wasn't an option. Each time I would say, "Yes, we do." She would hang up, and I would pray that she wouldn't show up.

"Dear Lord, she sounds so scary. Please don't let her come unless it's Your will," I would pray, seeking some peace of mind.

The strange calls came several weeks in a row, but she never followed through. I was starting to believe that she never would.

One Sunday as we were walking to Ocean City's Tabernacle for the morning service, a woman came toward us who actually gave me the willies. She was a large-framed woman with straggly blonde hair. Her white T-shirt was badly spotted with large dark brown chocolate stains. She was snaggle-toothed and wore dark sunglasses. A big, gold cross hung from her neck. As she passed by, I shuddered and silently prayed for her, as cold shivers traveled up and down my spine. The beautiful music coming from the Ocean City Tabernacle soothed my nerves as we approached the building. I tried to put the woman out of my mind.

The chambermaids usually go to the early service and then come back so that Larry and I can go to the second one. By the time we returned to the Logan that day, they had finished all the "change overs" and "make beds." So I started to prepare lunch for the crew.

Larry liked to leave for the trip back to Maryland by 2:00 p.m. on Sundays. The time between lunch and 2:00 went by entirely too quickly as far as I was concerned. After all the years of saying good-bye, it never gets any easier. Every Sunday, the wife in me wants to hold on to him and not let go. (It is the hardest time of the whole week.)

Reluctantly, I walked outside with Larry. The chambermaids who were leaving that day had already climbed into the back of the van. After kissing him good-bye and giving each of the girls a little thank-you note, I ran up to the landing to throw kisses and to wave until they were out of sight. (We usually have eight or nine girls working on the weekend, with five or six staying on to work during the week.)

It was such a beautiful day; I told the manager on duty to go to the beach with the rest of the girls. I really didn't mind taking the desk that afternoon.

There is something special about Sundays at the Logan. It's usually so quiet and peaceful. I love to play my praise tapes and bathe in the presence of the Lord. It's like soaking in a spiritual bubble bath!

The phone was ringing as I came back into the lobby. I ran over to the desk hoping that the person wouldn't hang up before I got there. Picking up the receiver, I heard that all-too familiar voice. "Do you have any rooms?"

I reluctantly told her that I did. " I'll be right there," she said, slamming down the receiver in my ear. There was an eerie feeling that came over me. I reassured myself once again, "She won't come. She never does!"

Putting in a praise tape, I started to clean up the kitchen.

The volume was up so loud that I barely heard the bell ringing at the front desk. I quickly wiped my hands on the kitchen towel I had draped over my shoulder. "I'll be right there," I said, totally unaware of who had come into the lobby.

THERE SHE STOOD. The screechy voice actually had a body and the body was wearing dark glasses, a chocolate-covered T-shirt, and a heavy gold cross! You guessed it, the lady we saw on the way to church and the witch-like woman on the phone were one and the same! I tried to remain calm. "You said on the phone that you had a room," she sneered. "How much is it?"

She held a folded newspaper up to her eyes to shield them from the light over the desk. *Boy, do I wish Larry was here now*, I thought as I showed her the rate sheet and told her the rates for the three different types of rooms. I could hear the music playing in the background. Strains of familiar choruses reminded me that I was not alone, but I couldn't help wondering what God was trying to teach me.

The unlikely guest turned her back and reached down the front of her shirt with her free hand and pulled out a wad of bills. She didn't realize that there was a mirror hanging opposite the desk on the wall by the door, causing her seemingly secret gesture to be in plain view. Turning once more and being careful to shield her eyes from the light, she threw the wad of bills onto the desk. "Now, give me the key to my room," she demanded.

So many thoughts raced through my head: *I'm so glad that I am on the desk and not one of my girls!...The other guests are really going to be afraid of her!...Even I'm afraid of her!... Help, Lord, what should I do?*

All of a sudden, I remembered something very important. "First, let me tell you a little bit about the Logan. We ask that there be no drinking or smoking. If you do smoke, you may do so on the porch. No outside guests are allowed in your room, and we ask that you whisper after 10:00 p.m. and before 9:00 a.m."

Before I could finish she said, "I don't want to hear all that! Just give me the keys!" (I was grateful that they were out of sight.) I was also glad that the lower half of my body was out of sight too (behind the desk). By this time my kneecaps were jumping up and down in a vertical direction.

"No one can stay here unless they agree to our rules," I said boldly, surprising myself. I realized once again that the rules were the Lord's smokescreen. And the smokescreen was working!

"I knew you just wanted my money," she accused, her voice getting more screechy as time went on.

Not missing a beat, I took the wad of money and gladly handed it back to her. "Oh no, ma'am," I said, "here's your money. I really think you will be happier somewhere else."

Still holding the paper up to the light with one hand, she grabbed her money with the other, turned around, and stuffed it back into her chocolate-covered shirt. I held my breath as she began slowly walking toward the door. I've never seen anything like it. It was like something in slow motion. When she got to the "welcome" mat, of all places, she turned, held out a crooked finger in my direction, and said haltingly, "You'll be sorry!"

"Lord, is she trying to put some kind of a curse on me?" I asked under my breath. "Well, I don't receive it, in Jesus' name! No amount of darkness can put out Your light!"

I expected her to go right out, but she stood on the mat, facing the door, and did the strangest thing. She started wiping off her feet–over and over again. This weird ritual lasted for about five minutes before she actually left.

Even though the incident left me shaken, I couldn't help being overwhelmed by what had taken place. I was awe-struck by the power of God against the enemy. Relieved that the ordeal was over, I collapsed onto the stool. "Thank You, Jesus," I said out loud. At that moment, I was pleasantly surprised to see one of our Logan guests come through the door. She walked directly over to where I was sitting. Great concern was written on her face.

"Joyce, I knew that woman was demonic when she first came onto the porch. I've been out there praying for you! Are you all right?"

"Yes, thank you so much for your prayers," I said, reaching over the desk to give her a big hug. God had done a tremendous thing in our midst. He delivered us from evil!

"Lord, You protect us all day long from the unseen world in ways we don't even know. Once in a while, You lift the curtain to allow us to see what's out there. We appreciate Your love and protection more than ever, knowing that You will never give us more than we can handle. No weapon that is formed against us shall prosper (see Is. 54:17). In Jesus' name we pray, amen."

Finally, be strong in the Lord, and in the strength of His might. Put on the full armor of God, that you may be able to stand firm against the schemes of the devil. For our struggle is not against flesh and blood, but against the rulers, against the powers, against the world forces of this darkness, against the spiritual forces of wickedness in the heavenly places (Ephesians 6:10-12).

Memories From the Attic

This past summer, 1998, I was blessed to be able to experience working and living at the Logan. Even though it was only for a few weeks, I feel permanently attached to the Logan and the people there. I feel like it is my second home! It was such an amazing time for me. I was able to serve God through the work we did, and I was able to witness, firsthand, the far-reaching ministry carried out at the Logan. Staying up in the attic, you could truly sense the girls who had stayed there in years past. It was so wonderful to enjoy fellowship with the other girls as we worked together. I definitely learned how to clean, and had so much fun in the process. We would sing songs and laugh together as we scrubbed and vacuumed. As beds were made and floors swept, lasting friendships were also formed. There is something very special about the Logan. It's as though God's presence was constantly pervading the air. I would definitely call it God's lighthouse for weary travelers!

Anna Burrows '98

I remember mending the torn cot mattresses. To motivate us, Joyce had a contest and gave out awards. I got the award for the mattress with the "most personality."

One of my favorite things to do at the Logan is to sit on the porch and talk to the guests. I enjoy seeing those guests who return year after year and meeting new ones.

Kathleen VanDerLinden '82-'98

Chapter 34

Homing Pigeons

For the Lord Himself will descend from heaven with a shout; with the voice of the archangel, and with the trumpet of God; and the dead in Christ shall rise first. Then we who are alive and remain shall be caught up together with them in the clouds to meet the Lord in the air, and thus we shall always be with the Lord (1 Thessalonians 4:16-17).

When I was a little girl, I had a pigeon named Henry. He had been injured and I had the joy of nursing him back to health. We lived in Washington, D.C., in an apartment house. Henry lived in a shoebox on the windowsill.

He flew away one day, and I never saw him again. (Perhaps if I had named him Homer, he would have stuck around or at least come back for visits.) He obviously was not a homing pigeon!

Almost 300 girls have flown in and out of the "Logan nest" over these 27 years. I try to avoid having perpetual *empty-nest syndrome*. To love them means I must be willing to let them fly away when the time comes. But it still hurts because each one flies out with a piece of my heart.

God has been so good, though, about bringing people back into our lives from the past. I think it must be part of our heavenly rewards here on earth. Every so often, the lobby door opens and in will walk a young lady with a familiar smile on her lips and sometimes a baby on her hips. I just love it when that happens! (My babies are having babies!) We anticipate having some second-generation Logan chambermaids this year for the first time ever!

As our girls are growing up in the natural, we especially love how they are growing up in the Lord. My favorite prayers for them are that "His word which goes forth from His mouth will not return void without accomplishing the purpose for which it was sent" (Is. 55:11, paraphrased); that "none of them would be lost" (Jn. 18:9, paraphrased); that God would raise up godly husbands for them; and that they "would bear fruit and their fruit would remain" (Jn. 15:16b, paraphrased).

Sometimes, my girls even come back to the Logan as guests and stay in their favorite rooms (the rooms that they used to clean and dream about coming back to one day). It's great that they still feel at home here.

Each one of our precious girls leaves a warm spot in the "nest" of our hearts that no one else can fill. As our "homing pigeons" fly in for periodic visits, I can't help but think about a time when we Christians will all fly *Home* to be with Jesus forever. What a day that will be! How the Father's heart must long to gather His children under His wings. I bet He has a *warm* spot just waiting for each and every one of us that no one else can fill.

"Dear Lord Jesus, how we long to be reunited with those we've come to love. It's so exciting when that happens! We really look forward to *flying Home* for a family reunion with our 'first love.' It will be a reunion that will make all other reunions pale in comparison. In Jesus' name we pray and anticipate that day, amen."

Memories From the Attic

Working at the Logan means "go around the tables," "jober-dos," sing-alongs, friends, Bible studies, and getting to hear Larry's infamous grunting! The Logan means a lot to me; it is a home away from home. For as long as I can remember I wanted to be a chambermaid there. When my family used to stay there during vacations, I would usually sleep in the attic with the chambermaids and help them with PB's (public bathrooms) and other dreaded jobs.

Now that I've been a Loganette for several years, I can look back and really see the spiritual growth and maturing that took place in my life through those many bliss-filled summers of independence. If it wasn't for my time at the Logan, I really don't know where or who I'd be now. My heartfelt thanks goes to Larry and Joyce for that opportunity.

Becky McDermitt '96-'98

Larry's "Hang Ten" apparel has always reminded me of the prints-in-the-sand story. It seems especially appropriate since the Logan is at the beach. I also think of a surfer catching waves. It brings to mind the Scripture about how the waves obey the Lord. God's peace is abundant at the Logan. I could feel it in the entire hotel. I really appreciate Larry and Joyce's desire to please and obey God concerning the Logan.

Melinda Kummer '98

Chapter 35

Special Delivery

And turning toward the woman, He said to Simon, "Do you see this woman? I entered your house; you gave Me no water for My feet, but she has wet My feet with her tears, and wiped them with her hair. You gave Me no kiss; but she, since the time I came in, has not ceased to kiss My feet. You did not anoint My head with oil, but she anointed My feet with perfume. For this reason I say to you, her sins, which are many, have been forgiven, for she loved much; but he who is forgiven little, loves little." And He said to her, "Your sins have been forgiven" (Luke 7:44-48).

I love it when God breaks into a normal kind of a day with a mighty demonstration of His miracle-working power.

It was an unseasonably warm January morning in Rockville, Maryland. The birds were chirping and the squirrels were scampering around in the backyard searching for hidden treasure. Signs of this pseudo spring were everywhere. I fixed myself a cup of piping hot tea and tried to find a clear spot on my dining room table.

Stacks of Logan mail, envelopes, and rate sheets literally covered every inch of work space. I carefully moved the reservation chart so that any unplanned spills wouldn't blot out any vital information. (One drop could be disastrous.) After turning on one of my favorite praise tapes, I proceeded to dive into the sea of paperwork. "This is a little overwhelming!" I said, trying to sing along with the tape to lift my spirits.

The shrill ringing of the phone startled me. "I wonder if I should just let the answering machine get that?" I debated. Sensing that it might be important, I ran to answer it before the machine picked it up.

"Hello," I said, trying not to sound preoccupied with the task at hand.

"Hello, Joyce, this is Nancy. I wonder if you could do me a big favor?"

Suddenly, the work in the dining room lost its importance.

"What can I do for you?" I asked my friend.

"Well, I guess you've heard that Martha is pregnant."

"Yes, Kristi told us. It must be very hard for all of you right now," I sympathized.

"Oh yes, it's been very hard. Martha is such a wonderful daughter. I had such high hopes for her. Sometimes life doesn't turn out the way you have planned. She refuses to marry Russ, the baby's father, because he isn't a Christian. We're proud of her for standing by her convictions. But, Joyce, she has become so withdrawn during these seven months. She feels so ashamed. Martha hardly ever goes out of the house anymore. When she does, she wears her big gray overcoat, refusing to take it off even when the weather is warm. She's even stopped going to church!" I could tell that Nancy was trying to hold back her tears.

"Oh, Nancy, my heart really breaks for Martha. Is there anything I can do?" I asked.

"Well, that's why I'm calling," she said with a little more hope. "I know you are busy working on the Logan mailing this time of the year. Is it possible that Martha could be of any help? She said that she was willing. Joyce, I really believe it would do her good to get out of the house."

"Of course," I said. "I'd love to have some help. I'll come by to pick her up in about an hour if that's okay."

"Yes," said Nancy, "that will be great. Thanks, Joyce. This means so much to me."

"Sure, I'm glad I can help. And it will be helping me too! See you shortly."

I was happy for the opportunity to see Martha again; she was such a sweet, sensitive girl and had always held a very special place in my heart. As I hung up the phone, I prayed, "Lord, please use me to show Martha how much You love her."

The day seemed "pregnant" with possibilities as I drove over to Martha's house. She must have been watching for me out the window. As soon as I pulled up, she came out the door. Sure enough, she was wrapped up in a big gray overcoat. Her long red hair shrouded her pretty young face. Jumping out of the van I met her halfway down the sidewalk. As I hugged her, I wondered if she could feel the warmth of my hug through the bulky material. She smiled weakly and said, "Thanks for coming to pick me up."

I opened the door to the van, and with a little effort, she climbed in. On the way back to my house the silence was broken by intermittent small talk. I tried to put her at ease. Before long, she seemed to relax. I was so grateful. Reassured of my unconditional love for her, she actually started to act like her fun-loving self again. Time flew as we worked on the mailing. It was like old times.

After the mailing was finished, I opened the door to the hall closet. Her coat felt so heavy as I handed it to her. "Do you mind if we swing by the post office on the way to your house?" I asked. "Not at all," she replied.

"By the way, Martha," I said as we got into the van, "I've been taking a class on hearing God's voice. Would you like me to tell you about it?"

"I'd love to know more about hearing God," she said, fastening the seat belt. During the ten-minute drive to the post office, I tried to condense the six-week course into a few main points. Like a thirsty little sponge, Martha soaked up every word. "Now, why don't you ask God if there is anything He'd like to say to you?" I was surprised at her response.

Her face became sullen as she said, "Oh no! I'm afraid He will tell me to give the baby up for adoption!" She wrapped her coat a little more tightly around her tummy, as if to press the little one closer to her heart.

"Martha, it doesn't mean He's going to say something that heavy. He might just want to say that He loves you."

Martha finally relented. She bowed her head. Praying that she would be able to hear God's voice, I anxiously waited for what seemed like many minutes. All of a sudden, Martha burst into tears. A flood of pent-up emotion erupted from her innermost being. I didn't know what to think. Her frail little shoulders shook violently as she buried her face in her hands. Looking back and forth from the road to Martha, I asked repeatedly, "What did He say? What did He say?"

Finally, Martha raised her head. Her long eyelashes were heavy with tears. Her face was radiant. Swallowing hard, she cried out triumphantly, "I'M FORGIVEN!" (The postman must have wondered why the Logan Hotel sent out so many soggy letters that afternoon.)

The rest of the way home we must have used up all the tissues I had sitting between the seats. We laughed and cried. We marveled at the goodness of our God.

What a wonderful day it had turned out to be!

The next Sunday, Martha came to church. With her head held high, she followed her mom and dad down the aisle. The radiance of God's love beamed from her face. It was such a chilly day, people might have thought that she had forgotten her coat. I knew better!

"Dear Lord Jesus, thank You that You are still in the business of setting the prisoners free. Help us to remember that Your blood cleanses us from *all* sin. 'There is therefore now no condemnation for those who are in Christ Jesus' (Rom. 8:1). As Martha shed her coat, she also shed her shame. God help us to do the same–in Jesus' name we pray, amen."

I waited patiently for the Lord; and He inclined to me, and heard my cry....And He put a new song in my mouth, a song of praise to our God; many will see and fear, and will trust in the Lord (Psalm 40:1,3).

* * *

Update!

Two months later Martha gave birth to a beautiful baby boy and named him Benjamin. She put her trust in God and waited patiently for Him while He worked in the heart of Russ, Ben's father. The following is an update written by Martha who continues to sing praises to her God for the things He has done.

"Russ accepted Christ as his Savior when Ben was two and a half years old. We were married a year later. We live in a small rural town. God blessed us with two more children, Rachel and Andrew. We are presently in the process of adopting a fourth child.

"God has been faithful to walk with us and sometimes to carry us through our journey in life. There have been many joys and some sorrows, but He remains faithful. For He who began a good work in each of us is faithful to complete it (see Phil. 1:6). He has made something beautiful out of our brokenness. May He be glorified!

"Two verses that have been very meaningful and helpful in our lives are: 'If we confess our sins, He is faithful and just to forgive us our sins, and to cleanse us from all unrighteousness' (1 Jn. 1:9 KJV); and ' "For I know the plans that I have for you," declares the Lord, "plans for welfare and not for calamity to give you a future and a hope" ' (Jer. 29:11).

"We thank God for the willingness of Christians to be used by Him to touch the lives of so many people.

Martha Cannon Lake"

Christ is in us, the hope of glory! (See Colossians 1:27.) Larry and I continue to give Him all the glory for the things He has done.

Memories From the Attic

I remember all the laughter and fun times we shared. Probably the thing that most stands out in my mind is dinnertime and Joyce's infamous, "Let's go around the table and everyone tell their most...time." That was usually followed by several "Ughs," but it was always fun–especially when the topic was for an "embarrassing" moment. It was always fun having Larry there on weekends. He would always have some funny comment or something to keep you laughing for awhile. I remember how he teased me so for the time I did my first laundry load when I was in manager training. I had never done laundry before and I guess I stuffed about three or four loads of sheets and towels into one. (The soap never got wet enough to dissolve.) He and Aunt Kay didn't let me forget that. I'm happy to say that I am much better with laundry now.

In closing, I'd like to thank Joyce and Larry for the opportunities they gave me at the Logan–first as a chambermaid and then as a manager. I have such fond memories of those days and of you all. I am grateful to Joyce for being the friend that she is and for giving me the gift of the Lord.

Jeanne (Ostrander) Cooper '83-'86

It was a day like any other at the Logan. When I vacuumed the front porch, I didn't notice that it was still soaking wet from the latest rainfall, so I vacuumed away, being sure to get every last crumb and bit of dirt. Moments later, I noticed large puffs of steam coming out of the vacuum bag, and I started to panic. Quickly turning off the vacuum, I ran to unplug it, and when I opened up the vacuum, the bag was full of wet dirt. I was so afraid I had killed the vacuum forever, and I thought of how terrible that would be when vacuums were so necessary to keep the hotel up and running. I dissected the poor machine and tried to sop up all the water. I worked quickly, anxiously waiting for Joyce and Larry to return from church so that I could give them the bad news. Fortunately, upon their return, Larry was able to help me repair the vacuum and get it running again. The ordeal ended with Joyce and Larry both telling me very gently to always "check the porch to make sure it's not wet before you vacuum." Ever since then, I have been extremely careful and cautious when vacuuming the front porch.

Jenny Parent '91-'99

Chapter 36

Father Abraham

Indeed I will greatly bless you, and I will greatly multiply your seed as the stars of the heavens, and as the sand which is on the seashore... (Genesis 22:17).

It may seem strange that I refer to my husband of 40 years as "Father Abraham." Let me explain.

Larry has looked like a football player ever since I first laid my 15-year-old eyes on him. He has big shoulders, big hands, big hugs, big smiles, big *toes*, and an especially big heart. He has a heart so big that it has embraced a multitude of kids over the 59 years of his life. Our wonderful children and their spouses and six grandchildren have more than blessed our quiver. One would have thought that would have been enough. But since we've been married God has brought 19 years of youth group kids under our wings. If that wasn't enough, He has also sent more than 300 chambermaids and managers into the Logan over the years for us to love (not to mention the countless young men and women who were guests as well). It makes our quiver shiver just to think of it.

That's where Abraham comes on the scene. It was Larry's birthday. I stood behind the Logan desk thanking

God for the wonderful man he had brought into my life. Not only had he been a shining example of a faithful, selfless servant; a wonderful husband, father, and grandfather; but he had become a second dad to many other kids. Children of all ages love Larry! Little ones like to climb him like a mountain, drape themselves over his shoulders, and sit on his lap. His strong arms have hugged hundreds and his big heart holds each one as his own, resulting in years of tears, agonizing prayers, and lots of joy–and the joy has been worth it all!

"Lord, thank You for giving Larry such a loving heart to be able to relate to these kids. He is like Father Abraham with so many children they outnumber the stars!" I said. I had looked at Larry as a Father Abraham for a long time, but on his birthday, of all days, the title was confirmed!

As I flipped the desk calendar to July 16, I was surprised to read the words God spoke to Abraham on Larry's very day, "...I will multiply thy seed as the stars of the heaven...because thou hast obeyed My voice" (Gen. 22:17-18 KJV). What a perfect birthday verse!

And while I made "Father Abraham's" favorite birthday cake that afternoon, yellow with chocolate icing, I kinda got the message that God looks at him that way too.

"Dear Lord, thank You for bringing such loving examples into our lives. May we also be faithful, selfless servants who always have room on our laps and in our quivers for one more blessing. As we commit to love, pray, and obey, please send spiritual children our way. In Jesus' name we pray, amen."

Memories From the Attic

What does the Logan bring to mind? My first impressions were made going up and meeting Mr. and Mrs. Meyer who showed us how to make "hospital corners" on the beds and "vash the vindows." I remember learning how to run down the steps from the attic to the third floor without breaking my neck. I saw the growth process in myself from a very self-centered, hot-tempered, 15-year-old girl to a more even-keeled, 22-year-old Christ follower and an almost-ready-to-be-married woman. This process evidenced itself in so many ways. I went from not really caring about the Scripture put at the top of each day's worksheet to being excited about reading the Scripture, from probably going through the motions of being at the morning Bible study to getting out of bed ready to participate and delve into the Scriptures, from just getting through the work to hit the beach to making sure everything was done–even if it took until 4:00 p.m.

At the Logan, I learned not only was it important to do a job well, but also to do it with the right attitude. I remember the times that I would be fuming at having to do a job over, but by the time I had finished redoing Room 8's shower, toilet, and sink I would have had my attitude realigned to "doing my work heartily as unto the Lord" (see Col. 2:23). I also saw that we not only lived out Christianity with word and tongue, but also in deed and truth (see 1 Jn. 3:18).

Ellen (Scroggs) Walton '73-'79

Chapter 37

Equally Yoked

Be ye not unequally yoked together with unbelievers: for what fellowship hath righteousness with unrighteousness? and what communion hath light with darkness? (2 Corinthians 6:14 KJV).

As I once discussed the importance of being "equally yoked" with my girls, one of them said that she used to think the verse "had something to do with eggs." I was surprised at how many of my chambermaids were unfamiliar with that verse.

The following summer, I came equipped with a visual aide. It was a snapshot of a yoke hanging on the wall of a barn. The girls could see by the shape of it that the oxen had to walk side by side after it was placed around their necks. Yoked together, they were inseparable.

I believe that the Lord wants us to be of one heart and mind with the people we are the closest to–such as in marriage, business partnerships, and in close friendships.

Can two walk together, except they be agreed? (Amos 3:3 KJV)

A story comes to mind that illustrates this point perfectly. I've always encouraged my Logan girls to date Christians to keep from being pulled away from Jesus, their first love. Ellen Scroggs was one of our first Logan managers in the mid '70's. She believed that only dating Christians was God's best for her. When Kip Walton asked her out, she thought that he was a Christian. It didn't take long for her to find out that he didn't have a personal relationship with the Lord. Being true to her convictions, Ellen broke off her relationship with Kip.

Now, when we were home in Rockville in the wintertime, Larry and I would regularly drive a van full of teens to a large gathering of believers in Washington, D.C. The beautiful worship and dynamic Bible teaching made us hungry for more. Ellen Scroggs was one of the teens who accompanied us on our weekly spiritual adventure.

One Tuesday night, Ellen received the shock of her life as she walked past a bank of bleachers. As she looked up in the center section, there sat Kip with a Bible in his lap. He was so absorbed in it that he hardly noticed Ellen trying to get his attention. You guessed it. The Lord had apprehended this handsome young man and brought him into the Kingdom "for such a time as this" (see Esther 4:14).

I can still see Kip leading Ellen in premarital Bible studies at the kitchen table at the Logan, practicing his role as the priest of the home.

We go to a lot of weddings. One year, there were nine in a three-month period. (And all three Rice girls married within one year.) Each wedding of our Logan Ladies is special and thrilling to Larry and me. We get the blessing of being another set of parents without having to pay the bills!

Kip and Ellen's wedding was worth waiting for. As I sat watching the ceremony, I marveled at the blessing it was to witness God yoking Ellen with Kip Walton. Great is God's faithfulness!

I still tell my girls at the Logan about the importance of being equally yoked so that the other person doesn't pull them away from their devotion to Christ. Now to go along with the picture of a yoke on the side of a barn, I have a real, live example. I tell them the story about Ellen, a person who loved and trusted her God enough to do things His way. Yes, God honored Ellen's faithfulness to be yoked with Him first, and then He led her to a godly mate–one He had picked out for her since the beginning of time. And when the timing was right, she found out who it was!

"Lord, being unequally yoked loses its appeal when it draws us away from the One who loves us most. You call us to take Your yoke upon us. That yoke of gentleness beckons us to learn Your humble ways, knowing that You have our best interests in mind. After experiencing divine union with You, it's a 'pain in the neck' to go our own rebellious way. Your offer is an engraved invitation with a promise that we gladly accept! In Jesus' name we pray, amen."

Take My yoke upon you, and learn from Me, for I am gentle and humble in heart; and you shall find rest for your souls. For My yoke is easy, and My load is light (Matthew 11:29-30).

Memories From the Attic

I remember that our week pretty much started when Larry took the orange van back to Rockville and we would sit around the kitchen talking to each other and visiting with the guests. Then we would go through each day with some mini crisis such as the laundry not delivering the pressed sheets, the washer breaking down, wondering if we had enough reservations for the upcoming weekend. We all looked forward to Friday when Larry would come back with "new girls." After unpacking the van, Larry would enlist us to help make the mega fruit salad, and we would get the new girls settled in up in the attic. Saturday nights at 8:00 or 9:00 p.m. we would all gather out on the porch with our song-books and guitars, and we would sing until 10:00 p.m.

Now these are some of the funnier incidents I remember: Robin and I picking Joyce up and placing her in the pan of soapy dish-water (I really can't remember why we did that!); Robin and I staying up until midnight while we waited for Joyce to finish witnessing to the lady in Apartment C so that we could lock up the place for the night (but then Joyce gave us the morning off and we biked down to Fifty-Fifth Street); biking down Ninth Street as I balanced two gallons of paint on the handlebars; Joyce answering the phone, "Hello, the Ocean"; either my brother Scott or Chip putting an elbow into a cereal bowl full of milk during one of the morning Bible studies (it kind of blew the deep theological discussion we were having!); Larry repeatedly telling me that I sounded like a "herd of turtles" coming down the steps; and Sue's all-protein mega-bucks diet that I followed for at least one meal.

There isn't enough time to recount all the great times I had at the Logan, so I'd better stop now. In Christ,

Ellen (Scroggs) Walton '73-'79

The Logan is such a special place of peace and growth in my memories. There are too many special memories to single out just one. To me, the Logan is like an ocean of diamonds glistening in the sun. You have probably seen this at one time in your life–it is the time in the morning when the sun hits the ocean just right and it looks like it is filled with diamonds. It's breathtaking! The sight of it is almost indescribable! This is how I feel about the Logan. There are so many beautiful diamonds in my Logan memories, all of which glisten from the light of the Son! I was able to meet the One whom I worshiped there. I was able to experience Him, to feel Him, and to listen to Him. I realized how beautiful and stunning my "Husband" really is. There have been very few places in my life where I have felt my Lord's presence so close and so real as I have at the Logan. How priceless are my precious diamonds from that beautiful place!

Jennie Allen '90-'97

Chapter 38

One Tick at a Time

My times are in Thy hand... (Psalm 31:15a).

And He has said to me, "My grace is sufficient for you..." (2 Corinthians 12:9).

I know my times are in God's hands, but I still need His grace one tick at a time.

Here's a behind-the-scenes look at some of the times God's grace was sufficient in the life of the Logan:

There was the time a man *just so happened* to be passing by at 5:00 a.m. and saw the awning next door ablaze (only five feet away from ours). Kids in the neighboring dormer had thrown lit cigarette butts out the window during the night. The man woke us up by yelling and banging loudly on our doors. To this day we are grateful for God's protection, fire extinguishers, the Ocean City Fire Department, and a man who went out for an early morning cup of coffee and became a hero.

There was the time I had asked one of our guests to turn on our coffeepot as she left the next morning. I awoke expecting to smell freshly made coffee and seeing the red light beckoning early risers to drink their fill. I was disappointed on both counts. "She must have forgotten," I concluded, tightening the sash on my robe. Since the coffee had been prepared the night before, I flipped the switch to the "on" position. For some *strange reason,* I touched the wire where it entered into the coffeepot. It was red hot! Had the lady remembered, I would have had more than a burn on my hands!

> *The angel of the Lord encamps around those who fear Him, and rescues them* (Psalm 34:7).

There have been the times that our blind friends, Lloyd and Judy, have ventured to New Jersey from Maryland on the bus. They frolic in the waves, walk the boards holding on to each other with one hand and their white canes with the other, and find their way back to the Logan every time. They might not be able to see in the natural, but their faith enables them to see deeply into the things of God– "...things which eye has not seen and ear has not heard, and which have not entered the heart of man, all that God has prepared for those who love Him" (1 Cor. 2:9).

There was the time that the golfers checked out and left five rings in Apartment A's bathtub. (Guess you could call us a five-ring hotel!)

There was the time I hung up the pay phone and quarters poured into our "quarters." (For a moment, I thought I was in Atlantic City.)

There was the time the seagull secretly flew off with the man's funnel cake when he turned to speak to his wife.

There was the time a fluttering bird gave the girls in the attic a "rude awakening."

There was the time the FBI surrounded the guest house down the street, confirming the fact that our sunny city doesn't cater to shady characters!

There was the time a hermit crab went into hiding in our front apartment, only to resurface four weekly rentals later.

There was the time a lady came down to watch the evening news in her underwear (covered by a long skirt hiked up to her armpits).

There was the time that I was cooling a watermelon on the windowsill and it took a "turn for the worse," giving new meaning to the word *splat*. (Thank God no one was on the driveway below!)

There was the time one of the girls fell down the attic steps and banged into Room 18's door (and they thought someone was trying to break in).

There was the time a little old man came down the lobby steps carrying a beach chair, dressed in his beach hat and underdrawers. (And Dad said, "Excuse me, sir, did you forget something?")

There was the time that the commercial laundry burned down and not one Logan sheet happened to be there.

There was the time that I checked in what I thought was a mentally challenged couple, who turned out to be high on drugs, and there was the time that we asked them to leave and I thought the lady was going to punch me in the nose!

There were the times we held rooms for people and they never showed up.

There were the times we turned people away for those same empty rooms.

There was the time that we laid hands on the washing machine and God miraculously healed it....

There was the time that the sewer backed up in the showers and a Christian plumber "bailed" us out. Ugh!

There was the time someone stole $60 from our little change bowl behind the desk.

There was the time I had a bad dream and screamed so loudly that the guests thought someone had been mugged in the alley.

There was the time the old gas oven in Apartment C blew off a lady's eyebrows.

There was the time a trash can was used to prop open the window screen in Room 10, and the driveway below Room 10 was full of trash (and we wondered why).

There was the time that the lady next door sat under the porch in her "birthday suit" (and all along I thought that it was a beige outfit).

There was the time someone closed the bathroom door and ran to get a plunger for an overflowing toilet (and the doorknob came off in his hand)!

There was the time we got the "alarming" news that we didn't pass fire inspection because of a technicality.

There have been the many times we've had to turn away unmarried couples.

There was the time that it rained all day and a little boy entertained himself by making "tinkle" designs on the bath mat.

There was the time a plastic trash bag with a hole and coffee grounds "decked the halls" behind a very zealous chambermaid!

There was the time the attic roof leaked and we ran out of coffee cans.

There was the time Larry shingled the roof, five stories up! (And I almost broke out in shingles!)

There was the time the man came to the desk with soap suds on his earlobes complaining that there was no water pressure in his shower.

There was the time a man used the phone booth, in the first floor hall, as a dressing room.

There was the time a chambermaid left a bundle of dirty towels in a couple's room (and we wondered why they were so grouchy when they checked out the next day).

There was the time I went into Room 4 to wake up my son Chip and discovered I had checked someone else into that room the night before. (Talk about a rude awakening!)

There was the time the Windex bottle dropped from the third floor window.

There was the time I checked someone into the linen closet.

There was the time two unsuspecting chambermaids almost passed out in the hall when they ran into the Christian entertainer, Scott Wesley Brown. (They had just been listening to a tape of his only moments before he checked in, which added to the thrill of the moment.)

There was the time the folding cot folded up with someone in it. (I was so glad it was a family member.)

There was the time the tuba player rented the apartment next door....

There was the time someone cleaned the kitchen floor with undiluted Ivory liquid dish soap. (The more she tried to rinse it off, the soapier it got.)

There was the time a chambermaid vacuumed up a guest's jockey shorts, and he walked in on her desperate attempt to disengage them from the power nozzle. (For a "brief" moment she wished she hadn't been so thorough.)

There was the time I ran with arms open wide to hug a long lost friend, only to realize that I had never seen the person before in my life.

There were the times my kids walked way ahead of me on the boardwalk. (I couldn't understand why; I was only skipping.)

There have been those times that the toilet water "rises to the occasion" and people keep on flushing.

There are those times when we've had to remind fun-loving guests to whisper after 10:00 p.m.

There was that time the scent of honeysuckle blew in the back doors and (you guessed it) set off the fire alarms.

There was the time a lady put on her aerosol deodorant out in the fourth floor hall and also got some "alarming results"—not to mention the French lady who popped her head out of Room 21 yelling, "Where's the fi-ure, where's the fi-ure?"

There have been the times we've had to pick chewing gum out of the green grass carpet on the porch with a dinner fork.

There have been the times that scary people wanted to check in and I wanted to check out!

There was the time a guest left several children in the lobby all afternoon while she took a nap upstairs and then got mad at me when I asked her to come down and tend to her children.

There was the time a chambermaid cleaned the mirrors with Pledgewood polish.

There was the time someone "streaked" from one shower stall to another.

There was the time the chambermaid bent over to put on her pants and broke the attic window with her rear end (Plexiglas to the rescue).

There was the time a very enthusiastic vacuum "cleaner" knocked a fire extinguisher off the wall and it too went into action.

There have been the times we've had to ask people to turn off T.V. programs that don't glorify the Lord.

There was the time some overly confident teenagers got swept out to sea by a riptide. (They came back looking pale and exhausted with a new respect for the ocean.)

There was the time a two-year-old pushed his stroller up to Wonderland Pier without either parent. (No wonder;

each thought that he was taking a little stroll with the other one.)

There was the time a squirrel broke through the screen of Apartment C and helped himself to the brownies and Johnson's popcorn by the window (while a guest slept peacefully in the same room unaware of her furry-tailed intruder).

There was the time a little girl locked herself in the bathroom and couldn't get out.

There was the time a man "helped" me back out of the driveway. (I still get embarrassed when people ask, "What happened to the fence?")

There was the Fourth of July when there was "no room in the inn" and a couple slept on the dining room floor.

There was the time the neighborhood cats thought our porch was a litter box.

There was the time I ran through the rain in tennis shoes that had just been washed in Ivory liquid soap the night before. (Have you ever seen soggy sneakers frothing at the mouth?)

There was the time the men replaced the front steps of the Logan and our three-year-old grandson fell 12 feet to cement below. He landed flat on his back surrounded by sharp tools and equipment. As the medics carried Anthony to the waiting ambulance, I ran to get my grandson's source of security, a plastic sword (that he never went anywhere without). Words cannot express the feeling I had when I saw the ambulance drive off with him lying on that stretcher holding onto his sword for dear life. My legs turn to Jell-O every time I think of it.

After a thorough examination in the emergency room, he returned to the Logan with only a slight concussion. Praise God!

I am thrilled to say, five years later, that Anthony finds his source of security to be a different type of sword–God's

Word. The Sword of the Spirit is something that he never goes anywhere without!

And then there was the time Larry said, "If you ever decide to sell this place, let me know." And I thought he was kidding! For how else would we have discovered that His grace is so sufficient ("one tick at a time")?

"Dear Lord, how we just love those fireside chats, sitting with a scrapbook on our laps, caressing grace-laced memories of times gone by that cause us to laugh, gasp, and cry. After all these years of knowing You, we can't help but think that You love them too–in Jesus' name we pray, amen."

Memories From the Attic

Independence came knocking at my door,
It said would you like to work this summer at the New Jersey shore?
I struggled as I considered taking the job,
For I knew that a lot of time from home and friends it would rob.
My uneasy decision was that I would chambermaid,
But after seeing the beautiful blue beach, all the uneasiness left me, and I was no longer afraid.
The boardwalk was awesome,
With the smells of hot oily fries, cheesy pizza, fattening funnel cakes, and then some.
The air was also filled with many sounds,
Like little ones whining and people laughing as my new friends and I walked joyfully around.
My family really missed me while I was gone, but when I was home we all got along.
Looking back, this freedom was a really good thing,
With all the friends I made, the closer I became to God, the money I earned, and the small tan I got, I feel like a king!
When asked to work again next summer I know my answer will be,
"I'm so excited you called! I'm ready to go! Will you please take me!"

Kimberly Avera '98

A unique feature about the Logan experience was the fact that only ladies worked there. This was a healthy aspect of growing up at the Logan; there were no guys to distract one's devotion to helping the hotel, or more importantly, to learning about Jesus.

Each summer I worked there I called my "convent summers" because of this.

My main exposure to men there was found in three forms: Granddad Oliveri (Joyce's Dad), Robby, and Larry.

Granddad Oliveri was a rigid man from the old school of thought when I first met him. But I kissed him on the cheek once and discovered that he was quite a charmer. This chivalrous gentleman liked to take us girls out to lunch. I loved his deep, velvet voice when he sang hymns.

Robby was the hotel mascot, I think. Robby was the big brother for all us Loganettes. He'd take us waterskiing or surfing if we wanted. (I personally forsook the pleasure of the latter.) The Logan would not be the Logan without Robby.

During the summers at the beach, Larry was my second father. His characteristic grunts and grumbles grew on all the Logan girls. Larry worked like a bull. He could often be found balancing or dangling from high, narrow, or otherwise dangerous places to the chagrin of his worried wife who jokingly threatened to go shopping every time he did such scary things.

Logan guests became like family as you saw them year after year. It was a thrill to hear the front desk bell ring and see a family one year older, especially if they had grown.

There were the teary times too. I saw some marriages dissolve and heard widows mourn. These were the times I learned to be a friend and not just an employee. If it were up to me, the Eastern Shore would be peppered with "Logan L'Abris"–it's a great place for employees and guests.

Whenever I returned home from the Logan, I usually slept for several days. Working there was always a privilege. Its responsibilities did take a toll, though. I always wondered how Joyce found solace at the hotel. Her Room 5 was directly across from the front desk. It was like Grand Central Station sometimes. The dreamer in me wished for her a large spacious room, high in the clouds that she could run to whenever things got overwhelming.

Emily McDermitt '87-'98

Chapter 39

The Captain

Then they cried to the Lord in their trouble, and He brought them out of their distresses. He caused the storm to be still, so that the waves of the sea were hushed. Then they were glad because they were quiet; so He guided them to their desired haven (Psalm 107:28-30).

No ship ever sailed without its captain. Ours was Dad. He was there helping me to navigate the Logan from the very beginning. Only two months before he sailed into his "desired haven," he could be seen sitting in his favorite chair on the "deck" of the Logan. Even at the age of 81, he still seemed to be at the helm wearing his navy blue, gold-braided captain's hat. His presence has been sorely missed. Many of you who came to know and love him might be interested in the events leading up to his final voyage September of 1996. The next chapter, "The Two-Legged Race to Heaven," will give the details of God's faithfulness as we went through those turbulent waters.

Since his departure, Dad's gold-braided hat still hangs by the door as a constant reminder that Jesus, the Captain of our souls, is still at the helm. He safely guides us through every storm and eventually, in His time, into the harbor of our heavenly home.

Before moving on let's take a look into the log book at some of my journal entries prior to my dad's departure.

- *Logged in the summer of 1995*: "A very zealous Messianic Jew came up to Dad and me on the sidewalk as we came down Sixth Street today. He asked Dad, "When you go to Heaven, what will you say to God?" (Up until that time, Dad had indicated that he didn't think that he was "good enough" to go to Heaven.) I loved it when he replied, 'Why, I would say, "Here I am, God! May I please see my wife?" ' What a day that will be! Lord, prepare him to meet You, to sing sweet bass notes to Your name, to embrace Your provision and Your grace and not be afraid of death when the time comes. Open wide the gates of Heaven, dear Jesus, that Dad may enter in! I entrust my dad to You."
- *Logged in January of 1996*: "Dear Lord, thank You so much for Your goodness and mercy. Incline Your ear to my cry for help for Dad. Father, please spare him from the devastating effects of neuropathy and diabetes. I pray that he will never lose his eyesight or a limb. Give him a new heart. Lord Jesus, take him to Your bosom quickly so that he won't have to go through anything worse. Hold him close and shield him from harm. Thank You for working Your angels overtime to keep him from falling (see Ps. 91:12). Please take away the waves of fear that try to engulf him at times...I commit him into Your hands."
- *Logged in February of 1996*: "Larry, Dad, and I watched *Touched by an Angel* tonight and it was about the passing of a patriarch. God, are You

starting to prepare us for what is to come? Is Dad going to die soon? I know our times are always in Your hands (see Ps. 31:15). Lord, You have Your hand on Daddy's life and his walls are ever before You (see Is. 49:16b). His birth and death dates are already recorded in Your Book of Life."

- *Logged in March of 1996*: "Lord Jesus, I believe that birth and death are very much like the day of Your return. You said we won't know the day or the hour, but we will know the season. Is this the season for Dad?...His arms look so thin today, Lord. He wears his watch halfway up to his elbow. We laughed about how high it would eventually get. He flexed his upper arm muscle and said that it would be up there soon. Thank You for his sense of humor. He has complimented every nurse that has come through the door of his hospital room. I'm sure that the morale on his floor will be boosted during his stay here. Perhaps that's one of Your purposes for Dad's many trips to the hospital this winter."
- *Summer of 1996*: "In my quiet time I turned to 'The end of all things is at hand' (1 Pet. 4:7a). Is this Scripture concerning the endtimes or my dad? Either way, I know that we don't have to fear the approaching storms...."

"Dear Captain of our souls, thank You for preparing us to sail through the storms of life. You will never send us into the storm alone. How comforting it is to know that You are at the helm. We look forward to the day that we, too, will be guided into

our 'desired haven'–in Jesus' name
we pray, amen."

Now, I'm excited to have the opportunity to share "The Two-Legged Race to Heaven," an incredible story of Dad's journey into the haven of his heavenly home....

Chapter 40

The Two-Legged Race to Heaven

...and let us run with endurance the race that is set before us (Hebrews 12:1).

For years, I had prayed that my diabetic dad would not lose a limb or his eyesight. I had trusted God on many other occasions, but this time, I really had to white-knuckle His faithfulness!

Mom died on Easter Sunday, 1991. Dad was devastated. They had been married for 56 years. I grieved for my mom, but I knew she was with God. The joy of knowing that swallowed up my sorrow. I grieved for Dad's loss even more. If only he could find his comfort in the arms of God.

Even though he was lonely, deep down, he wanted to stay in his home as long as possible. I was so glad that Larry and I lived close enough to watch after him.

The memory of that overcast day in January of '96 continues to surface on the screen of my mind like a rerun movie. A record-breaking snowstorm was expected. I felt uneasy about Dad being in his home alone. I remember carrying his groceries up the steps that day. The door was unlocked. Pushing it open, I found Dad sitting in his La-Z-Boy chair, as usual, watching T.V. Neuropathy had so numbed his lower extremities that his bare feet didn't even detect the winter chill. As I bent down to kiss his unshaven face, I was shocked to see that his feet were swollen to twice their normal size. I knew he was retaining fluid.

After a call to the doctor to get some advice, I quickly packed him up and took him to our home on Baffin Bay Lane in Rockville. That was the last time Dad was ever in his house.

The blizzard of '96 was only the beginning of many "storms" that our family experienced that year.

The doctor increased Dad's diuretic. He lost 20 pounds in three days! The sudden weight loss caused stroke-like symptoms. I was so glad Dad was with us and not alone. Almost three feet of snow held us captive for four days. Emergency vehicles could never have reached our house on the unplowed roads. God's presence became our strength during that scary time when Dad's health was so poor. Needless to say, the snowplows were a welcome sight on the fifth day.

During the next four months, the neighbors grew accustomed to seeing ambulances at our house. (Dad made nine trips to the emergency room!)

During one of his regular visits to the podiatrist, we received another shock. "It's dry gangrene," the doctor said as he looked at his infected toe. "We will need to keep a close eye on it. The toe will turn black and eventually fall off on it's own." (No one looked forward to that happening!)

During the days that followed, Larry and I took turns dressing his wound. He was such a good patient that it was a privilege to care for him. (I believe the Lord still washes feet today. He just uses our hands.)

My biggest challenge was to prepare food so that Daddy would enjoy it. The doctor took him off of salt because of his edema. Dad had grown accustomed to using so much of it that his food looked like the "White Cliffs of Dover." When he had to go "cold turkey," he had a terrible time getting used to it. To compensate, I tried using garlic powder, onions, and lots of green pepper to give his food some flavor. I bought more green peppers during that time than I had purchased in all my years of being a homemaker! Making Dad's food taste good almost became an obsession! The aroma of sauteed peppers constantly filled the air, permeating my clothes and hair.

Just to give you a little example, Larry stayed with him while I went to my weekly Bible study one Tuesday morning. Dotty Schmitt, our teacher, asked us to recite the twenty-third Psalm in unison. I joined in. "The Lord is my shepherd, I shall not want. He makes me lie down in green peppers!" I actually said, "Green peppers!" My face flushed with embarrassment. I guess, subconsciously, I was still back in my kitchen cooking for Daddy! (How important it is for caregivers to get away from it all and soak up the Word of God, even if, on occasion, they do forget exactly what it says.)

As the summer approached, I went back to innkeeping on the New Jersey shore. Dad loved staying with me at the Logan. Larry would shuttle him back and forth to Maryland for necessary doctors' appointments. (There were many.)

When he and Larry arrived the first Friday in August, Dad looked particularly tired. After a brief rest, he decided to go to the boardwalk on his electric (Rascal) scooter. The scooter gave him a sense of freedom since he had given up driving his car. He would wave at vendors and enjoy the ocean breezes as he scooted by. I was so grateful he could still see well enough to do this.

"Bye, Daddy, be careful," I called after him.

"I'll be back soon," he said as he rode up the sidewalk. I watched until Dad's "chariot" faded out of sight as he turned the corner at Wonderland Pier at the end of Sixth Street. I busied myself with hotel matters and tried not to be too concerned about him. "Lord, I love him so much, but I do need to let go and trust You to take care of him," I prayed. Before long, Dad returned looking pale and feeling sick to his stomach. We helped him out of the Rascal and sat him on a bench in the alley. One of the girls ran for a blanket. Checking him over I found that he was burning up with a fever and his blood sugar was elevated. Once again, we called 911. The ambulance took him to Shore Memorial Hospital in Somer's Point on the mainland.

"We'll have to keep him overnight because he is septic," the nurse said. "The infection from his gangrenous toe has invaded the blood stream."

"Overnight" became many nights. The unfolding of each new day brought an increasing awareness that Dad was not going to get well. Waves of mourning washed over the shores of my heart. I turned to my Bible to find comfort. A verse from Isaiah 60:20 made me wonder: "...the days of your mourning will be finished." The words seemed to jump right off the page. But the doctors continued to seem hopeful that Dad would pull through this.

"Lord, are You saying that Daddy will soon be going Home?" I had peace in my heart that he would go to Heaven when he died. The previous Easter, Dad and I had been watching *The 700 Club*, and Pat Robertson was praying the sinner's prayer. I asked Dad if he had ever invited Jesus into his heart to be his Savior and Lord. Indicating that he had never done that, I asked him to pray with me. He did. What a sweet privilege it was to pray with Daddy. (This was another pocket of blessing that God tucked into the folds of my life.) The enemy did try to rob me of that blessing by suggesting that he had only prayed to please me, but my peace remained.

I treasured each fleeting moment I had with Daddy. My heart ached as I left the hospital each day. The Logan was bustling with business at that time of the year, so I could only get over to the mainland once or twice a day.

The nursing staff was so kind to me. They never seemed to mind late phone calls to check on his well-being so that I could sleep peacefully each night.

With each passing day, I could sense that he was slipping away. "What do people do without God to get them through the storms in life?" I asked myself time and time again. Then, I'd sing quietly to the Lord as I walked down the lonely hospital corridors. The smell of flowers mingled with antiseptics became very familiar to me. Unlike Dad, I was free to step through the automatic doors into the warm sunshine. As I filled my lungs with the fresh ocean air, my eyes filled with tears. I felt so sorry for those who had lost the opportunity to do so.

One morning, I called to talk to Dad. After several rings, he finally picked up the phone.

"Good morning, Dad, how are you today?"

"Joyce, it was hell last night!" he answered, using words I hadn't heard him use for a long time. He didn't elaborate so I just thought that he had a bad night. I discovered later that someone else had called him that same morning. He had described his night to her in great detail:

> "I started screaming and the nurses ran in to calm me down. I spent the night in hell! It was dark and terribly hot! It was rotten and there were worms! No one should ever have to die like that!...Then, I saw the light! I knew it was Jesus! I CRIED OUT TO JESUS CHRIST MY LORD, AND HE SAVED ME!"

(God is so good. He's not willing for any to perish. See Second Peter 3:9.)

My heart leapt as I listened to my friend describe his story to me. I knew it was more than a dream!

Several days later, Dad saw men in biblical robes laughing and walking down the road. "I knew one was Jesus," he said. "He was in bright white!" I wondered at the time, *Where does the road lead and who are the people with Jesus?* Dad didn't say...I wish I had asked him.

We thought that we were prepared practically for Dad's death. He had a Living Will that had been signed in advance with his wishes fully known. Little did we know that it did not cover feeding tubes and resuscitation. The Lord once again prepared us for what was to come. One night I called to make sure Dad was stable and happened to talk to a Christian nurse. I asked her about the feeding tubes and resuscitation not being in the Living Will. She said that they were not covered automatically and that I needed to make Dad's wishes known regarding this because it would take an "act of Congress" to have them removed. I asked her to be sure that it was recorded on Dad's chart since it was his desire not to have these extraordinary procedures done to prolong his life.

The next night, Dad went into heart failure and I was called to the hospital. Not knowing what to expect, I "leaned on Jesus my Beloved" as I raced down the hall to Dad's room. He was gasping for breath under the oxygen mask. I peacefully sat by him on the bed and prayed and sang a few of his favorite hymns. At one point, he stopped gasping long enough to say the Lord's prayer. Then he put his mask back on and continued to struggle with each breath.

A cardiologist entered the room and said that he wanted permission to start the resuscitation procedure. I boldly, but respectfully, refused to give it. He said, "Do you know what you are saying?" as he called a nurse over to be a witness. In reply, I said, "When God is ready to take Dad to

Heaven, I don't want anything to stand in the way!" Normally, I would have been intimidated under such circumstances. It took a step of faith, but God had equipped me for the moment! After a couple of hours, Dad pulled through the crisis. (God extended his life long enough to fulfill His plan for him.) I left that night, marveling in God's faithfulness.

He spent a total of five weeks in the New Jersey hospital. Dad was four hours away from his own doctors; his only sister, Doris (who was in Maryland taking care of her sick husband, Norman); and his friends at church. "Could Dad possibly go back home for his last days?" I asked the Lord. Once again, God gave me the desires of my heart. It was just in time too. The doctors were ready to remove a portion of his gangrenous foot.

I sat up in bed one morning and heard the word "*Go*" loud and clear! It was the third of September. With permission from his doctor in Maryland, who cautioned that he may not survive the trip, I proceeded to make plans. If God had said "Go!" it would be worth the risk and expense to take him home. Two days and much red tape later, Dad and I, as well as an E.M.T. and a very nervous ambulance driver, who had never had anyone die in his care, were on our way to a hospital in Maryland. Dad slept most of the way. I was glad.

It was evening when we arrived. Dad's doctor met us there. After examining him, he came out into the hall to talk to me. The love for his patient of so many years was etched all over his grief-stricken face.

"I will be calling in a specialist. We may have to amputate his leg," he said sadly. Even though I was relieved that this caring friend was now in charge, those familiar words echoed in my ears and sent shivers down my spine.

Now, I had prayed Dad would never lose a limb, but sometimes God overrules my prayers. Perhaps this would be one of those times. I rehearsed the familiar phrase, "I must trust!" over and over again. Five doctors had decided that taking off Dad's leg would be the answer. I know that God honors those times when we submit to authority. It wasn't easy, but I agreed.

"Daddy, how do you feel about the surgery?" I asked. "Well, if the doctor thinks it's best, we might as well get it over with," he said with resignation and not much emotion.

I tossed and turned the night before Dad's scheduled amputation. The whole idea made me sick in my stomach. In my mind's eye, I remembered amputees who had courageously wheeled their way through my life. I never realized the valley of agony that they and their families must have endured as a result of their amputations. My heart was already grieving the loss of Dad's leg.

I really had to embrace God's faithfulness the morning of the surgery. Larry and I went to the hospital early so that we could see Dad before they took him upstairs. The peace of God that enveloped Dad astounded me. His friends, Robbie and Tom Smead, came to offer their support. We were so glad to have it.

The four of us accompanied Dad's stretcher as they wheeled him down the hall to the elevator. While the men sat in the waiting room, Robbie and I were allowed to accompany him to the O.R. holding room. We stood on either side of his bed and softly sang Dad's favorite hymns. The presence of God so filled the room that another patient even joined the chorus from a cubical near by. Dad hummed a few bass notes as he drifted in and out of peaceful sleep. They had not yet sedated him, so I knew this rest was a gift.

Someone had forgotten to order a chest X ray. They quickly wheeled in a portable machine. The (false) report indicated that he had pneumonia, so general anesthesia was out of the question. Taking him into the operating room, they resorted to a local anesthetic. Four times, they tried to put the needle into his spine. *Strategically placed* calcium deposits blocked their efforts. Three hours later, Dad returned to his hospital room with two legs!

There was no doubt about it—God had given us a sign—*a big stop sign!*

With a prognosis of about six months, Dad's doctor advised us to look for a nursing home where he would be made comfortable until the end. That evening, I turned on the radio. To my amazement, the song that was playing was "I'm Coming Home"! The one that immediately followed was "I'm Longing to Be Home"!

"Lord, this must be from You!" I said with tears cascading down my face. "Only You know the day and the hour of Daddy's homecoming." During my devotional reading that night I read, "Weeping may endure for a night, but joy cometh in the morning" (Ps. 30:5b KJV). It was the same verse that was inscribed on a mug that a Logan guest had given me just before I brought Daddy home. I sensed that his time was near!

I visited with Daddy a lot the next day while trying to find a nursing home in the area. I never told him what I was about. He never asked.

Sitting on the side of his bed that night, I whispered, "I love you, Daddy. It's getting late. I'd better be going!"

Dad looked lovingly at me through his cloudy blue eyes. He patted my hand and said, "I love you, honey...stay safe." Bending down to kiss his unshaven face, I gently tucked the covers around his frail body and said "good-bye." As I walked down the dimly lit hallway to the elevator, God impressed these words on my heart, "I was sick and you visited Me!" Now, in six weeks of hospital visits, I had never heard those words! Little did I know, it was a benediction!

Dad finished his race that night, September 14, 1996—with two legs! The joy of knowing he is safe in the arms of God swallows up my sorrow.

"Dear Abba Father, You whisper to Your children, 'I love you...stay safe.' Your words of comfort carry us through those dimly lit times when we lose our loved ones. The light of Your love engulfs our grief, bringing healing to our hurting hearts. The joy of knowing that we are safe in the comfort of Your arms swallows up our sorrow. In Jesus' name we pray, amen."

Memories From the Attic

When asked to relate my stories and memories from my days and hours at the Logan, words cannot express all that the Lord has shown me and taught me from my time resting in this godly haven. The responses I receive from telling others I worked at a hotel in Ocean City, New Jersey, for seven years usually run along the line, "Well, you must be a beach person," or "What a great place to work for the summer!" I laugh and tell them, "No, I could count on one hand the number of times I went to the beach during those seven years." Even after I explain why I worked all those summers cleaning rooms and managing the front desk, I don't think that they totally understand the love and gratitude I have for the time the Lord gave me to spend at the Logan. I see the Lord's sovereign hand in placing me at Church of the Atonement, where I would be in the Sunday school class of Larry and Joyce's daughter and where my mother would present me with the idea of working at a hotel during the summer. I think of the verse, "Being confident of this, that He who began a good work in you will carry it on to completion until the day of Christ Jesus" (Phil. 1:6 NIV). The Lord used my time at the Logan to carry on that good work, to chip off the rough edges and to continue the process of molding me into the image of Christ. He orchestrated the "utensils" for this fine-tune chipping through daily circumstances and through the lives of strong, faithful, and godly believers presented as role models to me.

Patricia Rice '90-'98

Chapter 41

His Story

Set up for yourself roadmarks, place for yourself guideposts; direct your mind to the highway, the way by which you went... (Jeremiah 31:21).

One of my favorite magazines of all times is *Guideposts*. I've read it for years. So many inspiring stories have jumped off the pages and hugged my heart. It's impossible to get through one without a box of tissues! I usually keep *Guideposts* right by my bed to read before I go to sleep at night. The most awesome adventures, like the ones where people are trapped under the ice, or fall down the side of a mountain, keep me on the edge of my seat (or should I say "bed"). Just when you think the stories can't get any better, they always do!

There's a reason I'm telling you all this. I want you to relate to my amazement when one of our guests who worked for *Guideposts Magazine* at the time urged me to send in a story about the Logan. Who in the world would want to read about a hotel on the Jersey shore? I asked myself. After much encouragement, I decided to meet the challenge. With a lot of help, the story came together.

Much to my amazement, "Life at the Logan" appeared in the August 1987 issue of *Guideposts*![1] And much to my surprise, the response was overwhelming. We received more than 50 letters and more than 100 phone calls from people who were touched by our story. Some of them even shared how they had cried when they read it. Some were encouraged as they related to our struggles. Do you believe it? People still call to make reservations more than ten years later, as a result of reading that article! We may have never fallen off a mountain or been trapped under the ice, but God can use His stories any way He wishes.

When we bought the Logan, we had no idea at the time that it was "His story" in the making! And to think, in high school, history had been my least favorite subject! You never know how God is going to work. Of course, He alone deserves the glory. After all, it's not about us. It is really about Him, which, in the long run, makes it His story!

"Dear Lord, it overwhelms us to think that our guideposts of yesterday can be used by You to guide others along life's highway. We stand amazed! In Jesus' name we pray, amen."

1. Joyce A. Coffin, "Life at the Logan," *Guideposts Magazine* (Carmel, New York: Guideposts, 1987), 24-28.

Memories From the "Male" Room

In the basement of the Logan is a laundry room. It is not just a laundry room; rather, it is the physical plant for the hotel, containing the behemoth boiler, washers, dryers, tool room, and towel and bedspread storage area. Tucked into this crowded space was my bunk. My Dad had fashioned a platform above the dirty laundry storage and below the mattress pads, large enough for a cot mattress and with enough room to lie down, but not enough room to sit up all the way. Directly next to my bunk was a cubby space where I stored my clothing and a really cool secret compartment where I could put my stuff. Between the hours of 11:00 p.m. (which is when the last load was done) and 7:00 a.m. (which is when the first load begins), this was my private space, my hideaway. There were not many private places in the Logan for a family or staff member. Most of life was spent in the company of others and although the laundry room was sometimes stiffingly hot, I would not have traded the privacy of that place for anything.

It was in the solitude of my bunk that I was introduced by my mom to a guest of the hotel using the laundry facilities. I was relaxing with a book shortly after graduating from dental school when I met Brenda Eifert. I knew immediately that she would be my wife. I had been a single dad for many years. I was starting a residency and entering a career. Love and marriage were the last things on my mind but the first things on God's. It was God's grace that smiled on me then, and I thank Him for the precious gift that she is. My children–Ben, Miles, and Kirk–have the ocean in their soul just as surely as sand sneaks its way into the plastic wrapping of one's lunch. My hope is that they will find the shore a symbol of God's grace as I have.

Lawrence "Chip" K. Coffin, Jr. '73-'81

Land's Edge Sacred Ground
...numbered grains
...named gulls
...stilled gales
Grace blows from the crests of winter waves
Whetting my heart's
Infant angles.

Lawrence "Chip" K. Coffin, Jr. '73-'81

Chapter 42

The Lighthouse Keeper's Kids

He makes the barren woman abide in the house as a joyful mother of children... (Psalm 113:9).

When Larry and I were dating, we went to see the movie, *Cheaper by the Dozen*. Our desire to have many children was *birthed* in that movie theater! Twelve sounded good to us!

Larry came from a family of nine children, so he was used to crowds. I have one sister, June (Oliveri) Bond, who is seven years younger than I am. After seven years of being an only child, I would have welcomed a crowd.

We had always loved working with children and looked forward to starting a big family as soon as we were married.

When that dream didn't come to fruition, depression came knocking at the door of my heart. I cried every time a baby commercial came on the T.V. As I watched little mothers strolling their babies down the street, I wondered what was wrong with me.

A three-month miscarriage only compounded the problem. After a while, we decided to put in for an adoption.

Finally, there was hope. Wading through endless red tape, the time had come for the agency to do a home study. As anxious as we were, we had to postpone it until after we returned from our two-week vacation in Florida. Much to our surprise, when we returned, I was pregnant! (Needless to say, we canceled the home study.)

April 22, 1963, at 6:22 a.m., Lawrence "Chip" Kirk Coffin, Jr., was born. We marveled at every hiccup and every yawn! He learned to talk and walk at an early age. Just after his first birthday, Chip stood looking sadly out the front door. He turned to me with tears in his eyes, and he said pitifully, "Mommy, I want a fwend." My heart melted. I didn't know if I could even get pregnant again. But, God's timing is always perfect.

Much to our amazement (15 days later than expected) on February 14, 1965, at 8:14 p.m., we received the most beautiful Valentine of all times. Our precious Kristi was born. Our faithful God provided a "fwend" for Chipper after all. (And it didn't take long for this forever "fwend" to become brother "Bipper's" little shadow.) God loves to grant the desires of even the smallest heart.

Back in the '60s, little was known about the Rh factor. We found out that Larry's O-positive and my O-negative blood was a bad combination. (In those days, they didn't know how to give shots to correct the problem like they do today.) We were in danger of life-threatening antibodies that could increase the risk with each pregnancy. A friend of ours had experienced the same problem, and she had to carry her dead baby for several months until she delivered naturally.

Not wanting to go through the same trauma, we gladly adjusted our teenaged dream of 12 children down to 2. God had given us a healthy boy and girl for whom we were so grateful. Having children was a dream come true, and we cherished every moment with them.

Larry, bless his heart, worked three jobs to enable me to be a stay-at-home mom. I wouldn't trade those times for anything in the world. God is so good.

This year, Chip is 36 and Kristi is 34. Where does the time go?

Chip, better known as Dr. Coffin in some circles, shares a dental practice with Dr. Don Davis in Lancaster, Pennsylvania. He has become a wonderful "Promise Keeper" husband and devoted dad. Chip is married to a precious, godly woman named Brenda Eifert Coffin who makes a perfect soul mate for him and wonderful "daughter-in-love" for us! She has put her career in clinical social work on hold to be a stay-at-home mom for now. They have three great boys, Ben, age 16, Miles, age 7, and Kirk, age 2 and a half.

Kristi is better known as "Mrs. Ivosevich" in her third-grade classroom as she teaches at Grace Academy, a Christian school, in Hagerstown, Maryland. She loves the Lord and is quite the "Proverbs 31" woman, and is a blessing to all who know her! Kristi is married to a wonderful guy named Mike who has his own construction company. Mike is a hard worker who loves God, his wife, and his kids with a passion. They have three great kids–Rosemary, age 11, Alison, age 10, and Anthony, age 8 and a half. (Boy, do we love being Granddad and Memaw to six terrific grandchildren!)

All of our children are surrounded by "fwends" without number. Chip and Kristi's families have no trouble practicing the gift of hospitality. I guess they come by it naturally after growing up at the Logan Hotel! I can still remember them setting the table when they were young, and asking, "How many for dinner tonight, Mom?" (Now their kids ask them!)

I thank God every day for my wonderful children. It's as if He gave us our heart's desires in the first place so He could fulfill those desires in the second place. Don't you love it when that happens?

It tickles me to think of how God had this all planned so many years ago. The once "barren woman" certainly has become a "joyful mother of (many) children"!

"Abba Father, some of us have known the heartache of being barren in body, soul, and spirit. When You bless our barrenness with fruitfulness, may we never get so busy being joyful that we forget to say, 'Thank You.' In Jesus' name we pray, amen."

Memories From the Attic

It is exciting to reflect back on all the memories. Now that I have a husband and family of my own, we are making new memories together each year at the Logan. My children love the bike riding we do on the boards; jumping the waves; making sand castles; walking on the beach searching for shells; enjoying the rides; playing miniature golf; singing on the front porch; and on the off-season, having the place to ourselves and playing an exciting game of hide-and-go-seek in the unoccupied building. To this day, if you ask them where they would like to go on vacation, they will tell you, "The Logan." It's our home away from home.

The most special thing of all has been growing up at the beach and watching my parents make a difference in so many young girls' and guests' lives. God has blessed them with this ministry, and I feel privileged to have been a part of the journey.

Kristi (Coffin) Ivosevich '73-'85

"The Logan"

A place to come and get some rest;
The beach–God's creation–one of His best.
Smell the fresh and salty air,
Relaxing vacations without a care.
A boardwalk and rides aren't far away,
For your enjoyment every day.
Sing-alongs on Saturday nights,
Will give you a break from the boardwalk's bright lights.
Riding bikes at the break of day,
Is a favorite pastime of those who come to stay.
Memories are made at the Logan each year,
And many lives are touched through its ministry dear.

Kristi (Coffin) Ivosevich '73-'85

Chapter 43

Patches

> *I will instruct you and teach you in the way which you should go; I will counsel you with My eye upon you* (Psalm 32:8).

Can we trust God's plan for our lives? Absolutely! When the children were little, God put this poem on my heart. It is just more evidence of the fact that He prepares us ahead of time for things that are to come. It doesn't mean we will always understand, but we can trust His ultimate plan (even if it includes lighthouse keeping!).

"A patchwork quilt sewn piece by piece, God plans your life for you,
Watch His handiwork increase in everything you do.
Some patches may not please the eye, or the colors don't seem true,
But only God knows the reasons why. He knows what's best for you.
The infant quilt is oh so small. A child drags his quilt behind.
The young man watches patterns fall, searching for design.

Maturity's view is more complete, as life's colors unfold,
But the total pattern cannot be seen 'til the thread is worn and old.
Then will patches spread before you, arranged by God's own hand.
The mysteries of life and living, you will start to understand.
In amazement, you'll discover, that through God's sovereign grace,
Mismatched patches you uncovered will have found a special place.
Your quilt is God's own masterpiece. Have faith and still believe,
In the loving design God plans for you with each patch that you receive."

"For I know the plans that I have for you," declares the Lord, "plans for welfare and not for calamity to give you a future and a hope. Then you will call upon Me and come and pray to Me, and I will listen to you. And you will seek Me and find Me, when you search for Me with all your heart. And I will be found by you," declares the Lord... (Jeremiah 29:11-14).

"Dear Lord Jesus, forgive us for not always trusting the work of Your hands. Thank You for the special plan that You have for each one of us. Thank You for working all our patches 'together for good' (see Rom. 8:28). In Jesus' name we pray, amen."

Memories From the Attic

The times I spent at the Logan will be special to me forever. There are so many lessons I learned and good memories that I could talk about, but I can remember one that has remained an important message from God throughout my life. I have always had some difficulty in life, and the Logan was the only place where I could be at peace. Joyce had always helped me by talking to me and praying with me, but I will never forget the time she said I reminded her of an old ship. At first I wasn't sure what she meant by that, but then she told me that old sunken ships were being brought back up from the ocean to be restored. The ships were covered with barnacles and had lost their luster. By the time someone took time to scrub off the barnacles and clean off the corrosion, a beautiful rare piece was created. She likened it to the many trials of life that harden your exterior, but once Jesus spends time cleaning all the harsh substances away, a beautiful person is evident beneath the tough exterior. I have never forgotten that analogy, and I know that the more time I spend with Jesus, the more His true nature will shine through me.

Denise G. Stang '85-'89,'92

Chapter 44

Lights

Again therefore Jesus spoke to them, saying, "I am the light of the world; he who follows Me shall not walk in the darkness, but shall have the light of life" (John 8:12).

All of us may not be called to be lighthouse keepers, but all are called to be keepers of His light. If we have invited the Light of the world to be our Savior and Lord, His light will automatically shine forth from our lives. (And no amount of darkness can snuff it out.)

Some people think that one person cannot make a difference in this world. I beg to differ.

During the ice storms in January 1999, we lost our power for a total of 42 hours. Tree limbs, heavy laden with ice, were breaking and crashing to the ground all around our Rockville home. Many of them fell on power lines. Explosions echoed through the darkness as traumatized transformers spewed splashes of light in every direction. The eerie sounds made for a rude awakening in the wee hours of the morning. Larry and I threw back the covers, jumped out of bed, and ran through the house in every direction, praying for God's protection. Finding the flashlight, I quickly dug out the matches and candles I had put aside for the possible Y2K crisis. The first candle I lit was placed on the kitchen table. The battery-operated clock in the kitchen said 5:10 a.m. As I placed candles throughout the house, I was amazed at how much light each candle produced. I had enough light to find things that had been lost in the darkness, and I was able to read my Bible in the candle's soft glow. That short time of distress put a new appreciation in my heart for the light (and heat) that I so often take for granted. It was amazing how one little candle could light up a big, dark room!

If one candle makes such a difference, what a greater difference many candles shining in the unity of God's love would make. No matter how dark things become in the world around us, His light will shine even brighter! It shines best against the backdrop of darkness.

This brings another story to mind.

A few years ago, Larry and I took a trip to Myrtle Beach with some friends to take advantage of an inexpensive January golf package. (Larry plays golf. I putter around.) We stayed on the ninth floor of a high rise right on the beach. The panoramic view from the windows was breathtaking. The first night we were there, I went into our room and closed the door. Turning out all the lights, I beheld the most beautiful, breathtaking sight. The stars, which looked close enough to touch, were so brilliant that they lit up the whole room. I stood there for what seemed like an eternity basking in the breathtaking beauty that had only been enhanced by the darkness. Then, it was as though the Holy Spirit dropped the following truth into my heart, "The darker the night becomes, the brighter My stars will shine."

When I returned home to Rockville, I went to the Olive Branch, a local Bible bookstore. There to my surprise I found a poster that had a dark blue background covered with bright twinkling stars. The message on the poster was very similar to the one I had received in Myrtle Beach. It was a confirmation to me that God was speaking loud and clear about shining for Him as the day of His coming draws near.

The following summer, I was sitting out on the back deck of the Logan having my morning devotions. I opened my Bible and was excited to find this verse:

> *Arise, shine; for your light has come, and the glory of the Lord has risen upon you. For behold, darkness will cover the earth, and deep darkness the peoples; but the Lord will rise upon you, and His glory will appear upon you. And nations will come to your light, and kings to the brightness of your rising* (Isaiah 60:1-3).

These seemingly prophetic words jumped right off the page and into my heart. Can you sense the urgency as well?

In light of the following Scriptures, how can we resist?

> *And this is the message we have heard from Him and announce to you, that God is light, and in Him there is no darkness at all. If we say that we have fellowship with Him and yet walk in the darkness, we lie and do not practice the truth; but if we walk in the light as He Himself is in the light, we have fellowship with one another, and the blood of Jesus His Son cleanses us from all sin* (1 John 1:5-7).

> *For Thou art my lamp, O Lord; and the Lord illumines my darkness* (2 Samuel 22:29).

> *Light arises in the darkness for the upright* (Psalm 112:4a).

> *Then your light will rise in darkness, and your gloom will become like midday* (Isaiah 58:10b).

And so we have the prophetic word made more sure, to which you do well to pay attention as to a lamp shining in a dark place, until the day dawns and the morning star arises in your hearts (2 Peter 1:19).

But you are a chosen race, a royal priesthood, a holy nation, a people for God's own possession, that you may proclaim the excellencies of Him who has called you out of darkness into His marvelous light (1 Peter 2:9).

For you were formerly darkness, but now you are light in the Lord; walk as children of light (for the fruit of the light consists in all goodness and righteousness and truth), trying to learn what is pleasing to the Lord. And do not participate in the unfruitful deeds of darkness, but instead even expose them; for it is disgraceful even to speak of the things which are done by them in secret. But all things become visible when they are exposed by the light, for everything that becomes visible is light (Ephesians 5:8-13).

"Dear Lord, it's amazing to see how You can take darkness and use it for a backdrop to enhance Your light. Help us to see the darkness as a blessing in disguise. Give us insight so we can arise and shine in all circumstances. In Jesus' name we pray, amen."

Memories From the Attic

Over the course of the past seven summers, I was blessed by the many Bible studies I participated in. We started out with some singing and prayers of adoration to the Lord. Joyce led the Bible studies and always chose a wide array of topics that pertained to the lives of teenage girls and young women. The Logan was truly a house of God. Each morning we prayed for God's peace and guidance in whatever situations we might face that day. We praised Him for the Logan and prayed that our lights would shine to all the guests and friends who passed through. Some highlights I can remember learning from the Bible studies are the names of God, the importance of blood covenants, and how to know when you have found the mate God has chosen for you to spend your life with. Our theme passage in the Bible was Proverbs 31, in which we were told how to be godly women and faithful, honorable wives. Joyce always called us her "Proverbs 31" women.

When I think of the Logan, my mind is filled with so many good memories and peaceful thoughts. What a haven this wonderful house has been to so many people over the years, including myself. As an employee, I had the most wonderful opportunity of working side by side with some of the greatest children of God you will ever meet. Not only did I enjoy the work and the people I worked with, but I was able to live at the beach all summer. I have always had a special love and passion for the ocean, where the power of God is so evident! The Father God has made the Logan what it is today. I have very fond memories of sing-alongs on the porch, Bible studies in the mornings, crazy times in the kitchen, and the laughter and tears we all have shared. So many friendships have been built there that will last a lifetime. I am so thankful for a place where people can go to rest in the peace of the Lord. It is a place of beauty and happiness. There are always so many smiles and "hellos." There is so much to do and so many ways to get involved. Favorite times include the Fourth of July celebrations, baby-sitting for some of the guests, and making dear friends with many of the frequently visiting guests. I grew so much as a Christian and as a woman at the Logan. I was taught to be responsible, patient, and loving when the circumstances told me to act otherwise. I had great practice at being a mother and a wife. Doing loads and loads of laundry taught me to be patient and responsible, and because I've always loved to cook, making dinner was always a good opportunity to improve on my culinary skills.

All these things make the Logan what it is today and what it has been in the past. More than anything, the love of the Lord shines through. Hundreds of lives, including mine, have been blessed by the Logan and have also been impacted by this great house of God.

Jenny Parent '91-'99

Chapter 45

Hindsight on High Places

You are the light of the world. A city set on a hill cannot be hidden. Nor do men light a lamp, and put it under the peck-measure, but on the lampstand; and it gives light to all who are in the house. Let your light shine before men in such a way that they may see your good works, and glorify your Father who is in heaven (Matthew 5:14-16).

From the vantage point of my Father's lap, I ponder the past 27 years of running His lighthouse. Just as early morning beachcombers retrace their steps to find every last treasure, I wander down the corridors of my memory extracting precious things from the past. If we had never bought the Logan, just think how many blessings we would have missed!

The Lord went before us and set the stage. He opened a door that no man could open. He met me at the end of my rope. He took me up on my invitation to make Him my Lord. He worked all things together for good (see Rom. 8:28). He absorbed my fears in His perfect love. He provided wonderfully-"maid" chambermaids and managers. He taught me the King-sized lesson to work as unto Him. He loved, prayed, and hugged through me. He found lost joy. He put miracles into my arms. He continues teaching me to praise Him in all things (even when falsely accused). He calls us to come unto Him when we are weak and heavy laden. He gives rest to the restless. He protects us from storms and night terrors. He gives us the privilege of beholding the Lamb. He makes me more appreciative of those I love. He lets me lean on Him during wilderness times. He is my very present help in trouble (see Ps. 46:1). He gives me practice to be a more cheerful giver. He tucks treasures into the pockets of my life. He guides me even when I'm not aware of it. He remembers my heartaches and tears. He reveals the things of darkness and brings them into the light. He shows me a wide "range" of blessings that can come from such a narrow kitchen. He makes lasting impressions on me through little people. He makes heavenly matches. I find His wisdom at my disposal. He heals grasshopper mentalities. He provides safety in the strong tower of His name. He's the lifter of our heads in times of trouble. He puts smiles on broken hearts. He delivers me from evil. He brings blessings back into the nest. He speaks words of forgiveness into our shame. He gave me a wonderful husband, who is sometimes known as "Father Abraham." He warns us about being unequally yoked. He gives the grace we need one tick at a time. He's the Captain of our souls. He gives us the endurance to run the race. He gives the joy of knowing when our loved ones are with Him. He urges us to set up guideposts along the way that become journal gems one day. He made this barren woman into a joyful mother of children (see Ps. 113:9). He is the great Designer who has a place for every patch. He has taken two unlikely people and made them the keepers of His lighthouse on the Jersey shore. He has taken the meager offering of this unlikely author and created a book. What a joy it has been to share His stories with you. Thankfulness streams from my heart to Jesus, the One who "is the same yesterday and today, yes and forever" (Heb. 13:8). To Him be the glory!

"Dear precious Lord, it's wonderful to know You are in control. We no longer have to be afraid to step through new doors of opportunity. Forgive our skid-marked thresholds of the past. In one way or the other, when the time is just right, make us all keepers of Your light. In Jesus' name we pray, amen."

Memories From the Attic

Working at the Logan was a growing point in my spiritual walk with the Lord. I learned the importance of starting out my day with God by having devotions and a quiet time (often by the ocean). During my quiet time, I learned the discipline of journaling. It was difficult at first to put my thoughts on paper and then write what I heard God saying to me. When prayers were answered, we were encouraged to put the date next to the request. At times as I look through my journal I marvel at how many prayers were answered. Now as a wife and mom, I especially know the importance of daily prayer. My experience at the Logan has taught me to persevere and know that God really answers prayer.

Jody (Sensenig) Detweiler '85-'90

The Logan is a lighthouse in this world, a vessel used on a mission field. At the Logan, the ministry is to us girls who come up to chambermaid and to each and every guest who walks through the front door. There are so many ways in which one can minister to others. The Lord used Larry and Joyce to teach me this–to use every opportunity for Him and seek ways in which I can serve the Lord with my life through the circumstances in which He has placed me. Living in that way makes one a full-time missionary!

Patricia Rice '90-'98

Chapter 46

May Our Lives Tell His Story

If you happen to be strolling down Sixth Street in Ocean City, New Jersey, on a Saturday night in the summertime between eight and nine, it's very possible that you will hear the "lighthouse keepers" singing one of their favorite songs. By this time, it is more than a song. It comes very close to describing the mission that was given them to fulfill 27 years ago by a very awesome God:

"Shine, Jesus, Shine"[1]
by Graham Kendrick

"Lord, the light of Your love is shining, in the midst of the darkness shining;
Jesus, Light of the World, shine upon us, set us free by the truth You now bring us,
Shine on me, shine on me.

---

1. SHINE JESUS SHINE by GRAHAM KENDRICK ©1987 Make Way Music (adm in N, S and C America by Integrity's Hosanna! Music)/ASCAP. All rights reserved. International copyright secured. Used by permission.

Chorus:
Shine, Jesus, shine, fill this land with the Father's glory;
Blaze, Spirit, blaze, set our hearts on fire.
Flow, river flow, flood the nations with grace and mercy:
Send forth Your Word, Lord, and let there be light.

Lord, I come to Your awesome presence, from the shadows into Your radiance;
By the blood I may enter Your brightness, search me, try me, consume all my darkness,
Shine on me, shine on me.

Chorus:
Shine, Jesus, shine, fill this land with the Father's glory;
Blaze, Spirit, blaze, set our hearts on fire.
Flow, river flow, flood the nations with grace and mercy:
Send forth Your Word, Lord, and let there be light.

As we gaze on Your kingly brightness, so our faces display Your likeness;
Ever changing from glory to glory, mirror'd here *may our lives tell Your story*,
Shine on me, shine on me.

Chorus:
Shine, Jesus, shine, fill this land with the Father's glory;
Blaze, Spirit, blaze, set our hearts on fire.
Flow, river flow, flood the nations with grace and mercy:
Send forth Your Word, Lord, and let there be light."

"Dear Lord, it's amazing to think that You took such ordinary people, put them in such an ordinary place, and brought about such extraordinary results. As we come under Your Lordship, may each one of our lives tell Your story in the days to come. 'Send forth Your Word, Lord, and let there be light'—in Jesus' name we pray, amen."

Now to Him who is able to do exceeding abundantly beyond all that we ask or think...to Him be the glory...forever and ever. Amen (Ephesians 3:20-21).

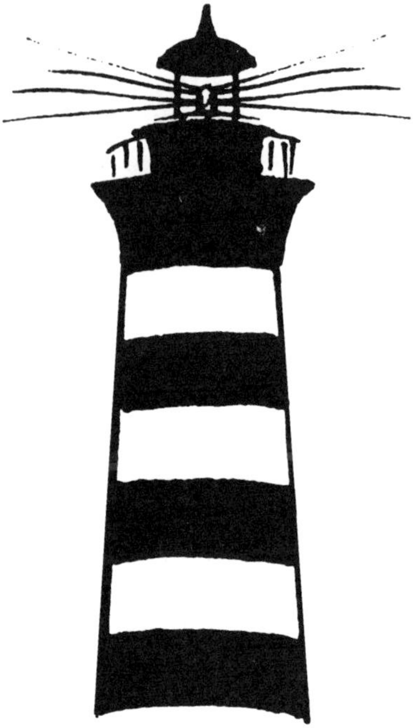

If you embrace a blessing today,
If my heart streams happen to flow your way,
If a beam from the Lighthouse has brightened your
  day,
Then, let's throw Jesus a big bouquet!